It's possible to change your life, and *Forbes'* "queen of manifesting" Roxie Nafousi is here to show you how to do it. *Manifest in Action* teaches readers how to unlock their limitless potential, create lasting, transformative change, and turn dreams into reality.

Providing practical techniques to expand readers' understanding of each of the seven steps to manifestation, *Manifest in Action* demonstrates how to harness your potential and confidently step into your power. Each chapter is filled with simple and inspiring exercises designed to cultivate self-awareness, reflection, and growth, empowering you to manifest the change you want to see in your life.

Described as "the face of manifesting" by *The Times* and "the voice manifestation needs" by Jay Shetty, Roxie Nafousi can help any reader find their way to empowerment and success in just seven simple steps.

MANIFEST IN ACTION: UNLOCK YOUR LIMITLESS POTENTIAL

MANIFEST IN ACTION: UNLOCK YOUR LIMITLESS POTENTIAL

ROXIE NAFOUSI

ST. MARTIN'S
ESSENTIALS
NEW YORK

Published in the United States by St. Martin's Essentials, an imprint of
St. Martin's Publishing Group

MANIFEST IN ACTION. Copyright © 2023 by Roxie Nafousi. All rights
reserved. Printed in the United States of America. For information,
address St. Martin's Publishing Group, 120 Broadway, New York, NY
10271.

www.stmartins.com

The Library of Congress Cataloging-in-Publication Data is available
upon request.

ISBN 978-1-250-34017-7 (paper over board)
ISBN 978-1-250-34018-4 (ebook)

Our books may be purchased in bulk for promotional, educational,
or business use. Please contact your local bookseller or the Macmillan
Corporate and Premium Sales Department at 1-800-221-7945, extension
5442, or by email at MacmillanSpecialMarkets@macmillan.com.

Originally published in the United Kingdom by Penguin Random
House UK.

First U.S. Edition: 2024

10 9 8 7 6 5 4 3 2 1

To Wade,

Thank you for teaching me so much, for your unconditional love, for supporting my manifesting journey, and for being the best dad in the world to our perfect little boy.

CONTENTS

INTRODUCTION

The night before we entered 2022, I sat down, as I do every year, to make my new-year vision board. I set the scene by lighting my favorite candles and then I lay down on my yoga mat and sank into a deep state of relaxation as I followed a guided visualization meditation. Afterward I got out a large sheet of card and started writing down, in detail, all the goals I had for the next year. I dreamt *big*. My debut book, *MANIFEST: 7 Steps to Living Your Best Life,* was six days away from release and of course I had some apprehension about how it would be received. (I would be lying if I said imposter syndrome wasn't something I was battling—*more on that later.*) But, taking my own advice, I made sure not to allow my fear and doubt to influence what I would put down on my vision board. I penned a heading, *the MANIFEST book,* and underneath it I wrote *Sunday Times bestseller, America, Vogue, multiple languages.* Nine days later, *MANIFEST* debuted at number five on the *Sunday Times* bestseller list (and as I write this now, it has remained on that list for the last sixteen weeks), a month later I signed with American publishing house Chronicle Prism to release the book in autumn 2022, and then shortly after that *British*

Vogue dedicated an entire article to the book and named it "2022's answer to *The Secret.*" Oh, and *MANIFEST* has been translated into seventeen languages *and counting*.

Can you imagine what my younger self would have thought of all this? I often think about that, and about the person I was less than four years ago: an extremely lost girl, battling addiction with zero self-worth, no career prospects, and who had never really known what it was like to be happy. I wonder what I would tell her. I think I would say this: **Life is wonderful and you have the power to make it so.**

It's hard to put into words how the last few months have felt. It's as though I've been thrust into a magical whirlwind, fueled by manifestation, and the response to, and reach of, my little orange book has been completely mind-blowing. Manifesting is a practice that means so much to me, one that has transformed my life beyond recognition. I live and breathe the steps that I teach, and I wholeheartedly believe they have the power to transform the lives of anybody and everybody that follows them. I am honored, humbled, and in a permanent state of deep gratitude that I have been able to share what I have learned with so many of you.

While my first book *MANIFEST* was the introduction to my unique seven-step guide to manifesting, in this

book you will *dive deeper* into the inner healing required to really unlock your limitless potential. I will be
presenting new ideas and concepts to help expand your
understanding of the practice, and also answering some
of the questions I have been asked most frequently. For
example, *why should I put my vision board away? How do I
stop caring so much about what other people will think? Do I
have to be positive all the time to manifest the things I want?
How do I know the difference between a test from the universe
and a sign that I need to change direction?*

What makes this book so unique, though, is that it
is also *filled* with practical exercises for you to complete, which will encourage the self-reflection, self-
awareness, and clarity needed to empower and *up-level*
your manifestation practice. I encourage you to work
through this book slowly, taking your time with each
exercise and giving yourself the space and opportunity
to feel the effects of them. By the time you reach the
final page, you will have a greater understanding of
yourself and what you really want from your life, and
you will have begun healing parts of yourself that you
may never have even known needed healing. You will
be living more authentically, you will be manifesting
powerfully and effortlessly, and you will know what
you need to do to ensure that you are living a life that
finally brings you the contentment and fulfillment that
you so deserve.

I may have been the author of *MANIFEST*, and my name may sit on the cover of this one, but as you dive deeper into my seven steps to manifesting and work through the exercises provided, *you* will be required to become the writer and storyteller. You will learn how to be your own healer, your own guru, and in doing so you really will become the author of your own story. What could be more powerful than that?

KEY MANIFESTING TERMS

The universe

When I refer to "the universe" throughout this book, I am referring to an energetic force greater than ourselves. For me it is the universe that holds the power and magic behind manifesting that is greater than our conscious awareness. If, for you, this energetic power is something different, then please feel free to replace "the universe" with your own interpretation at any time throughout the book.

High-vibe

An abbreviation for *high-vibrational frequency*. The law of attraction states that like attracts like, so if we are vibrating at a high frequency, we will attract things that match that high-vibrational frequency.

Low-vibe

An abbreviation for *low-vibrational frequency*. If we are vibrating at a low frequency, we will attract things that match that low-vibrational frequency.

Abundant mindset

A belief that there is more than enough for us all. This mindset helps us keep attracting abundance into our life.

Scarcity mindset

A belief that there is not enough for everyone. It creates a constant feeling of lack and hinders our ability to attract abundance.

STEP 1

BE CLEAR IN YOUR VISION

"Everything you can imagine is real."

PABLO PICASSO

OVERVIEW OF STEP 1

- You can't get to where you want to go if you don't know where you are heading. So, before anything else, you must first decide what it is you really want.
- You must try to gain as much clarity as possible around what it is you want to manifest. Being vague simply won't be enough. *The more details the better!*
- If you don't know exactly what it is that you want, think about how you want your life to *feel*. You can manifest a feeling.
- Visualization (*creating a mental image of the future using your imagination*) is a powerful manifesting tool that will help you reach your goals more easily. This is backed by neuroscience; research has found that regularly visualizing your goals will help your subconscious work toward reaching them by filtering out unwanted information and seeking opportunities that are in line with that imagined reality.
- When visualizing the things you want, immerse yourself in the feeling of having them. For example, if you want to manifest your dream home, visualize the details of the house and then immerse yourself

in the feeling of walking through the front door. *We attract what we feel.*

○ The most important question of your manifesting journey is this: *who do you want to become?* When visualizing your future self, visualize the highest and most empowered version of yourself. Know that this version of yourself already exists; it's dormant but waiting to be unleashed as you follow my seven-step guide to unlocking the power of manifestation.

○ A vision board is a visual representation of how you want your life to be, and I encourage everyone to make a vision board to mark the beginning of their manifesting journeys.

○ Dream big and don't hold back.

Thinking about the future can be daunting and exciting, terrifying and exhilarating, all at once and in equal measure. When you try to imagine what you want your life to be like in a year, or five years from now, you may be able to instantly visualize all your dreams playing out like a movie in your mind with no hesitation, or you might feel like you are staring into an abyss of nothingness. When we think about what our future could hold for us, there is so much possibility, so much potential, and so much room for vast expansion. Yet there can also be so much fear, concern, and apprehension that comes with that. The fear presents itself as internal questions that ask **what if it doesn't happen** the way I want it to? Or what if I fail? Or even why can't I see what I want?

As we work through this step, I am going to ask you to let go of that fear, concern, and apprehension. Simply set it aside. Right now, all you need to do is come with me as we open your mind's eye (*your imagination*) to your future so that we can replace that fear with excitement.

Before we begin, I think it's worth reminding ourselves of this: **manifesting is not just about attracting "things" into our lives or manifesting how we want our lives to *appear to others*. No, it is about manifesting a life that makes us feel content and fulfilled, and one that allows us to experience joy, excitement, and love. Getting to the crux of what will bring you those feelings is the key.**

I recently hosted a workshop and during the Q & A, a woman asked me, "How do I even begin to figure out what I want? Sometimes I don't know the difference between what I really want and what I think I should want." I get it. It is so easy to get trapped in the idea that we should all want the same thing. We can feel pressured to say, or feel, that we want to get married and have children and live happily ever after with one person forever, or that we want to have an impressive job title that's high-pressure but comes with a six-figure salary and a company car. But the truth is, that's not for everyone. Not everyone wants to have those things and *nor should they*. Isn't it time we gave ourselves permission to figure out what we actually want, instead of allowing the pressures of society to dictate it for us? Isn't it time we gave each other that permission too? It's OK if you don't want children; it's OK that you don't want to start your own company in an age of freelance; it's OK if you don't feel the need for a fancy job title; it's OK if you crave nothing more than simplicity; it's OK if you want to go slow rather than race through life. Basically, what I'm saying is that it's OK to want whatever it is *you* really want, and just because that's different from what anyone else wants, *or what you may have wanted in the past*, it doesn't make it any less valid, exciting, valuable, or inspiring.

DON'T BE AFRAID TO SHINE IN YOUR UNIQUENESS AND LIVE LIFE ON YOUR OWN TERMS.

To help the woman in the workshop understand what she *really, authentically wanted*, I first asked her this: when did you feel most content, fulfilled, and at peace? What were you doing at those times? Who was around you? What else was going on in your life at that time? When you think about the answers to those questions, you can start to get to the core of what makes you feel happiest. You can use those memories as clues. Then you can begin to cultivate and manifest more of that into your life.

✏️ EXERCISE

Before we go on, I'd like you to answer these questions for yourself:

> Describe when you felt most content, fulfilled, and at peace. What were you doing, who was around you?

. . . .

. . . .

. . . .

. . . .

. . . .

. . . .

. . . .

. . . .

. . . .

. . . .

. . . .

. . . .

. . . .

. . . .

....

....

....

....

....

....

....

....

Using your answer as a guide, now answer these two
questions:

1. What clues does that memory give you about what
you want to manifest?

....

....

....

....

....

....

....

....

....

....

....

....

2. Are there things in your life that are blocking you from experiencing that contentment, fulfillment, and joy more often?

....
....
....
....
....
....
....
....
....
....
....
....

I love doing this exercise myself, and I come back to it often. In the hecticness of life, reflecting on what *actually* makes me happy is so important. It reminds me to cultivate more time for simplicity and to stop chasing things that I think I should want or that I used to want. In doing so, it also helps me to live in greater alignment with who I truly am. Also, by recognizing what is currently blocking me from experiencing those feelings more often, I am able to identify which areas of my life I want to change and what, perhaps, I need to let go of.

HOW DO YOU WANT TO FEEL?

If you're having trouble figuring out what it is you want, start instead by identifying how you want your life to feel. Remember that you can manifest a feeling. In the following exercise, identify how you want to *feel* within your life. To make this a little easier, let's categorize our lives in four main areas:

1. love & relationships
2. career/work
3. home/day-to-day
4. experiences/leisure

➡ EXERCISE

For each category write down any words or phrases that describe how you most want to feel in this area of your life. For example: joyful/at peace/safe/comfortable/confident/empowered/respected/valued/excited/inspired/organized/challenged/stimulated.

LOVE & RELATIONSHIPS	HOME/DAY-TO-DAY
CAREER/WORK	EXPERIENCES/LEISURE

You can use **the answers to help guide your under-standing of what you can specifically manifest to cultivate those feelings.** For example, if you want to feel a greater sense of peace in your home life, then you could use that to inform what kind of environment you'd like to create for yourself. Or if you want to feel challenged and stimulated in your career, then perhaps consider whether the career path you are currently on can provide that for you, or whether there is something else that may be more aligned with those feelings?

The intention of this exercise is to help you clarify how you want to feel within different areas of your life and to use that to offer greater clarity on what you want to manifest. I suggest that now, using this as a starting point, you **create a vision board.**

Vision boards

A vision board is a visual representation of what you want your life to look like. For me it is an integral part of this first step. It is an opportunity for us to paint the picture of our lives and get crystal clear on what specific dreams, hopes, and desires we want to manifest, and *when* we want that to happen by.

In *MANIFEST* I shared a vision board guide, and I am resharing the steps here for when you are ready to make your new vision board. What I ask of you, though, is to really challenge yourself to write down *everything* you want to attract into your life and be mindful of any time you are being held back by your fear and doubt. Every time you go to write something on your vision board, ask yourself these three questions:

1. Could I dream bigger?
2. Is this something that will fulfill me and cultivate the feelings I want my life to be filled with?
3. Is this completely authentic to my own desires, dreams, and wants?

If you've created a vision board already, but it doesn't accurately represent your deepest and wildest dreams—now is your chance to make a new one.

Creating your vision board

1. Set the scene

Light some candles, play some relaxing music, and create a calm and meditative environment. Make your vision-boarding exercise a sacred event for you to enjoy and indulge yourself in.

2. Choose your medium

Take a large sheet of card or paper and choose whether you prefer to write down your goals using different colored pens (either in bullet points or as a free-flowing description) or whether you want to use images (draw them yourself or cut out pictures or words from magazines or newspapers that reflect the things you want to draw into your life).

Choose whatever feels best for you—just remember to have fun with it.

3. Choose your timeline

At the top of the page, write the exact date by which you want to manifest what's on your vision board.

You could choose to do a six-month, one-year, or even a five-year vision board. Personally I like to do all three.

I sometimes find that people can struggle to know, and visualize, what they want their life to look like one year ahead, yet they may feel much more able to visualize their lives in five years' time, or vice versa. So if you are feeling a little stuck, remember you can always choose a different timeline.

4. Get in the zone

Before you start adding things on to your board, make sure you are already embodying the feeling of your future self. Pause for a moment, take a few deep breaths, and imagine yourself exactly six months, or one year or five years, from now. Create a clear and vivid image in your mind as you ask yourself the following questions:

- How do I feel within myself?
- What kind of relationships surround me?
- What kind of home do I live in?
- What is my profession?
- What am I most proud of?
- What do I want to change in my life?
- What do I want to keep the same?

As you answer these questions, allow yourself to be completely free in your dreams, desires, and wants. Do not allow fear to hold back your imagination; instead, take your mind's eye to the exact place that you want to be. Allow the image of your future self to really come to life as you sink into that visualization.

5. Separate your life into categories[1]

Split your vision board into six categories:

- Personal development (i.e. your personal growth/ how you want to feel within yourself)
- Love and romance
- Career
- Friends and family
- House/home
- Hobbies/leisure

6. Design your life

For each category, write down all the things that you want to manifest within it. If you are using cut-out images, such as an image of your dream house, stick them on to your vision board.

I would try to have a minimum of three things per category, but there is no limit on how many things you can add to your vision board!

---

1   This step is optional. I love to do this, because it helps me clarify what I want in all areas of my life, rather than focusing in on just one part.

BE CLEAR IN YOUR VISION

21

7. Put it away

After creating your vision board, put it away somewhere safe and set a reminder to come back to it on the date you wrote at the top.

WHY DO YOU PUT YOUR VISION BOARD AWAY?

This is probably the question I get asked the most, probably because there are other experts in this field who suggest keeping your vision board somewhere you can see it every day, so the conflicting advice can be confusing. Let me first say that there is a good argument for both sides and I am certainly not trying to say my way is the only way; I will explain my reasoning, but ultimately you should decide what feels best for you.

The first reason why I suggest putting your vision board away is this: to manifest anything into your life you need to know what you want (*be clear in your vision*) and then you need to surrender to the journey that will lead you there. Step 7: Trust in the Universe is about cultivating the feeling that you don't know *how*, but you just know that it *will* happen the way it's supposed to; it is this high-vibrational confidence and assuredness that leaves no room for doubt to exist. You are not trying to *force* things into place, as this can be accompanied by a low-vibrational, desperate, and distrusting energy. No, instead, you are simply doing the things you can day-to-day (i.e. following the other steps and committing to your inner healing journey to remove fear and doubt, aligning your behavior, or overcoming tests from the universe) and then trusting, unwaveringly, that it *will* happen. Putting your vision board away is, to me, a physical and symbolic representation of this; you write down what you want and then, by putting it away, you are surrendering to the journey of manifesting.

I also believe that if you were to look at your vision board every day, it would risk taking you away from **the manifesting sweet spot** (described in Step 5: Embrace Gratitude (Without Caveats)): **knowing where you want to go while being entirely grateful for all that you already have.** It's just not possible to be as present, mindful, and grateful for all that you already have if every day you are looking at your future goals and wondering how and when they will be achieved.

Another reason I suggest putting your vision board away is this: your vision board should be a sacred, honest, vulnerable representation of all the things you want to manifest into your life. You want to write down *exactly* how you want your life to look and feel, and to allow yourself to be honest about your deepest desires. If you have your vision board on show, for example as your phone screen saver or on your wall, I wonder if you would really put down all your most authentic dreams; you may not be as brave or as honest about the things you want to manifest because, perhaps even on a sub-conscious level, you will be holding yourself back in case someone else sees it.

So here's what I suggest doing: make your vision board with absolutely everything you want to manifest into your life in precise detail, allowing yourself to dream big, being completely honest and vulnerable with what you really want to attract to your life, and make it authentic to you. **When it is complete, put it away somewhere safe.** Then if you want some sort of visual representation that you can have as your screen saver or on your walls to *inspire* you day-to-day, **make a MOOD BOARD.** A mood board can be made up of pictures or words that represent what you want your life to feel like and the kinds of things you want to manifest into your life, but without the specific details.

FAQ:

Q: Should I be realistic when creating my vision board or deciding what I want to manifest?

A: NO! The minute we start trying to be "realis-tic," we are allowing ourselves to be restricted by our fears and doubt. Step 2: Remove Fear and Doubt is integral to every step of the process, including this one. You must decide what life you really want—not what life you think you can realistically make for yourself.

Your vision board is not a place for you to play it safe; it's for you to expand the limits of your mind and therefore the limits of your reality.

YOUR PERFECT DAY

As well as making a vision board, visualization is another practical way for you to work through the first of my seven steps to manifesting. Sinking into a visualization meditation allows you to immerse yourself in the feelings of what you want, shifting your vibrational frequency and instantly influencing what you then attract to your life. There is a great quote from the bestselling author Bob Proctor that says, "**If you can see it in your mind, you can hold it in your hand.**" I always think of that before I go into any visualization.

I do a visualization meditation every night before I fall asleep. It is a ritual that helps me on my own personal journey and one that has become an effortless part of my daily routine. I either follow a guided meditation or I simply take myself into a relaxed state, focusing on the rise and fall of my belly while I inhale and exhale. I then take my mind's eye to my future and conjure as much detail as I can around a particular thing I want to manifest, *immersing myself in the feeling of already having it*. For example, when I wanted to manifest my goal of becoming a *Sunday Times* bestselling author, I would visualize myself opening the newspaper and seeing my name on the list, and then I would imagine how that would *feel*, immersing my whole being in feelings of joy, pride, and excitement.

However, like I am sure many of you have experienced while practicing visualization, there are times when I struggle to create a clear vision of what I want to manifest next. This can be because I am feeling a little uninspired that day, or because I am truly feeling content with all that I already have and I'm just not motivated to create new goals at that time (*after all, manifesting is about living your best life, not about relentlessly pursuing more, more, more!*). So **I wanted to find an alternative way to immerse myself in a high-vibrational feeling of the future without needing to constantly find a new goal to visualize.**

I started to do something a little different; I started to use my meditation time to picture and run through *my perfect day*. I would choose a time in the future, maybe a month or a year from now, and imagine everything I would do in that day from the moment I woke up to the moment I went to bed. At the start of the meditation I would decide on the location, the season, and the people I would have around me, and then I would go through the day in as much detail as possible. My perfect day is different almost every time I do this visualization, but I always think about which simple pleasures I would indulge in and conjure up feelings of contentment, joy, and gratitude. Sometimes I take myself on holiday, some days I imagine an inspiring and exciting day at work, and sometimes I just visualize a day with my son, Wolfe, filled with play, cuddles, and laughter. You can choose to vary your perfect day or run through the same one each time; all I ask is that you don't reflect on a perfect day you have already experienced—the day should be sometime in the future.

Should you wish to try this technique yourself, I have created a "Perfect Day" meditation as part of my collection of meditations and affirmation tracks available from my website, www.roxienafousi.com.

▣ EXERCISE

I love doing this as a journaling practice too, so, using the space on the opposite page, I want you to write down a detailed description of your perfect day. As with the meditation, take yourself through your perfect day, starting from the moment you wake up, and write the piece like a diary extract, as though it has already happened. For example, you may start with *Dear Diary, today was just the most perfect day. I woke up and the first thing I saw was the glorious blue sky outside my bedroom window . . .* Include as much detail as possible and remember to immerse yourself in the feeling of the experience as you do so.

Knowing how you want your life to feel, and what you want to attract to your life, will kickstart your manifesting journey. Incorporate visualization meditations as part of your daily or weekly routines and when you create your vision board, dream big and don't hold back. Remember: you are the author of your own story. When you think about your future, get excited because the best is yet to come.

My perfect day

....
....
....
....
....
....
....
....
....
....
....
....
....
....
....
....
....
....
....
....
....
....
....

BE CLEAR IN YOUR VISION

29

STEP 2

REMOVE FEAR AND DOUBT

*"You have to let it all go . . . Fear, doubt, and disbelief.
Free your mind."*

MORPHEUS, *THE MATRIX*

OVERVIEW OF STEP 2

○ We don't manifest from our conscious thoughts
   alone, but from our subconscious beliefs about what
   we deserve and from our self-worth.
○ Our feelings of fear and doubt are a culmination of
   our low self-worth, insecurities, limiting beliefs,
   conditioning, and past experiences.
○ Fear and doubt are the two things that stand in the
   way of us and our dreams.
○ Removing fear and doubt requires a commitment to
   inner work and to your healing journey. This is what
   makes manifestation such a transformative self-
   development practice.
○ This step is on-going, and the work required to
   remove the blocks of fear and doubt will be different
   for each person.
○ One of the ways you can begin to do this is by
   becoming aware of your conscious thoughts, because
   they influence what our subconscious believes to be
   true.
○ Mastering our thoughts, using mantras, switching
   our language, changing our perspectives, and using

visualization techniques are tools that we can use day-to-day to help us to do this.
  ○ To manifest anything into your life, you must first believe you are worthy of receiving it.

When writing *MANIFEST*, the most important lesson I had to communicate about manifestation was this: we can only manifest what we subconsciously believe we are worthy of, and the two things blocking us from having everything we desire most are *fear and doubt*. To attract the abundance of the universe we must begin to remove these blocks so that they no longer hold power over us. But our fears and doubts are built up over years and years, decades even, and they're not built like a tower that you can just bulldoze in one big push. Instead, it requires us to carefully, slowly, steadily remove each of the blocks one by one, in the process freeing ourselves from the weight of them.

I believe that we are born into this world full of confidence and unconditional self-love, but then something happens that strips us of that: *life*. Life happens. And somewhere along the way, little by little, we get stripped of that magnetic and powerful energy and our confidence gets replaced by self-doubt, limiting beliefs, and a feeling that we just aren't enough. Removing fear and doubt is really embarking on a journey back to ourselves.

I gave some examples in *MANIFEST* about how to begin the journey of removing fear and doubt day-to-day, such as using mantras, switching the language we use, and becoming masters of our own thoughts. In this book I want to delve deeper into the techniques that I have found to be incredibly effective in helping me remove fear and doubt, and which have guided me through my transformative healing journey.

HEAL THE WOUND, *NOT THE SYMPTOM*

I remember having a text conversation with my ex-boyfriend when we were bickering about something unimportant, and it was starting to get a little heated and escalating in the way these things often can. He said to me, *I can't engage with this anymore*. As soon as I read those words, my heart felt like it was shattering into a million pieces. I interpreted what he said as: *I can't be with you anymore*. What he said had triggered me. It caused feelings of rejection and abandonment that supported my limiting belief that I was unlovable. I responded to him by saying, *Fine, I guess we're over then*. He was rather stunned by my response, to say the least, because of course all he had meant was *I can't engage with this conversation anymore*, but what I had received was different. It was different because my interpretation was informed by my fears and doubts, by my past experiences and my subconscious beliefs. **In other words, my current reality was being restricted, limited, and controlled by my past.**

Whenever our old wounds are unhealed, we leave ourselves open to being triggered by them. How many times have you felt inexplicably hurt by something that, in hindsight, was quite insignificant? Or how many times have you said something to someone and felt they took what you said entirely the wrong way? **This is because our past experiences, and our fears and doubts, become the filter through which we experience the current moment, influencing our interpretations and the meanings we attach to them.**

What usually happens when we are triggered is that we try to heal the symptom. For example, after that conversation with my ex-boyfriend, and because I was not at a point in my self-development journey where I was aware that I was being triggered, I focused all my energy on trying to make the situation better (i.e. the symptom). I did this by making amends to clear the air with him so that we could carry on "as normal." I wasn't dealing with the source of the reaction (i.e. the wound) but the aftermath. How many times have you done that with a partner or friend? Can you remember an occasion when you just wanted to make things better and so brushed over everything that had happened and rushed to make up to avoid any more discomfort, instead of actually addressing the reason the disagreement or argument happened in the first place? When you did that, did you then end up fighting about the same thing again weeks or months later?

In hindsight, what I should have done was taken a second to consider my reaction and think, *OK, I've interpreted what he has said in a way that he didn't intend*, which I know because he has told me as much. *So where did my interpretation really come from? What past experience or wound was informing that reaction?* This would not only have helped me to let go of something that was having a subconscious hold over me *and lowering my vibration*, but it would also have helped to ensure that the same thing didn't happen again. This is also how we can take responsibility for our own "stuff" in relationships, which is key to the sustainability of any healthy relationship.

> TO BREAK PATTERNS OF THINKING AND BE-
> HAVIOUR, SO THAT WE AREN'T DICTATED TO
> AND CONTROLLED BY OUR PAST, WE MUST
> BECOME ACUTELY AWARE OF OUR WOUNDS
> AND BEGIN TO HEAL *THEM* RATHER THAN
> THE SYMPTOMS.

On my own healing journey, understanding that my reactions are not directly linked to the current situation, but almost always influenced by my past, has been an incredibly profound realization. I am constantly asking myself, "Where is this coming from?" so that I can let go of the control my past has over me. That is the inner work required to really master the practice of manifestation. **To unlock the most powerful, confident, and magnetic version of ourselves that exists, we must break free from the shackles of our past, and to do this *we must heal*.**

There is an idiom that I think sums up triggers quite well. I'm sure you've heard it before: *the straw that broke the camel's back*. The Collins Dictionary definition is: If an event is "the last straw" or "the straw that broke the camel's back," it is the latest in a series of unpleasant or undesirable events, and makes you feel that you cannot tolerate a situation any longer. To me triggers are the last straw in a series of undesirable events in your life that are being stored in your subconscious and which cause you to react or respond in a way that is disproportionate to the event you are currently experiencing.

I should preface this next part by saying that I understand that the wounds people have experienced during their lives will vary, and the severity of trauma caused will be different for each person. The healing journey you will be required to go on will therefore be unique to you. I am not claiming that these exercises will be the start and end of that journey, but they will help you to, at the very least, begin that process.

I am going to share how I have coped with triggers and healed my own wounds, but in full transparency I would also like to add that I did support this work by seeing a therapist. For anyone who feels their trauma, wounds, or past experiences are too challenging to face alone, please reach out for external and professional support—help is out there in many forms.

AWARENESS

"Emotion and cognition, undefined and unexplored, drive every decision you make. You either develop self-awareness or these things control you."

BRENÉ BROWN

The first step to healing any fear or doubt that may be hindering our manifesting abilities is to become aware of them. Triggers are brilliant indicators that *something is unresolved here,* and therefore they can help us see where fear and doubt may be lurking. I invite you to practice becoming acutely aware of when something is triggering you, which means paying attention to *any time* you feel angry, resentful, frustrated, sad, or anxious. When these feelings arise, I want you to pause to consider what triggered those feelings and to ask yourself whether your reaction was an appropriate response to the stimuli (*you will need to be honest with yourself here*) or whether it was being informed by old wounds. For example, if you received an email from your boss that was offering constructive criticism, and you felt immediately defensive or angry, ask yourself: is my reaction entirely warranted by the context of the email? Is there a chance I am misinterpreting the tone or intention behind it because of an old experience, belief, or fear? If the reaction is not warranted, you can begin to explore where that response *really* comes from. For example, did it conjure up feelings of never living up to the expectations of your parents or teachers at school? Or did it trigger a fear of rejection or a subconscious belief that if you are not "perfect," then you are not worthy of the position?

Awareness of our feelings, and therefore our triggers, offers us a powerful opportunity to zoom out and recognize that our narratives, thoughts, feelings, and interpretations are not necessarily aligned with what is *actually* happening. With awareness you can pause and ask yourself this very important question: "Can I be entirely certain that the negative narrative I am creating around this event is factually correct?" Often the answer is no; we have such limited insight into other people's intentions, thoughts, or feelings that we are constantly filling in the gaps and constructing our own stories and assumptions. This can work to serve us or to hinder us. When it is the latter, it is because these narratives are being informed by fear and doubt.

Here's another example. Let's say that you go to a friend's birthday dinner. At this dinner you find yourself feeling a little out of place because you aren't familiar with many of the other people attending. You arrive and start talking to one of the guests who the host introduced you to and a couple of minutes into the conversation they look over your shoulder and see that their friend has just arrived, so they excuse themselves and walk over to greet them. Your inner critic, *your voice of fear and doubt*, suddenly starts to bombard you with thoughts like, *They obviously thought I was boring. I'm no good at socializing. I shouldn't have come.* You immediately feel self-conscious, deflated, and awkward, and the rest of the evening is completely overshadowed by those feelings, negatively interfering with all your inter-actions with the other guests and encouraging you to leave at the earliest opportunity. In this instance, the trigger was someone ending a conversation with you to greet their friend. With awareness you could stop and ask yourself, "Is there actual evidence to support my assumption that this person left because I am boring or no good at social-izing?" The answer, of course, is no. Then you could try to identify what was influencing that narrative; you may realize that this experience has triggered the self-doubt you always feel when meeting new people. You may even remember specific examples of feeling unwelcome in a new environment. **This is where you could then begin your healing process.**

NO MATTER WHAT YOU ARE TRIGGERED BY, YOU MUST RECOGNIZE AND UNDERSTAND THAT IT IS ALWAYS BEING INFORMED BY YOUR YOUNGER SELF AND PAST EXPERI-ENCES.

You might be reading this now and wondering, *So how do we actually heal?* Well, the first thing to say is that the healing process begins the moment you are able to acknowledge that your past experiences and traumas are driving your reactions, perceptions, and narratives. By bringing past experiences to light, out from the dark depths of our subconscious, they no longer have the ability to unknowingly influence us. But we can also heal by using various self-development techniques that can help us to process and let go. Here are two that I use when I find myself feeling triggered by my past:

1. Journaling

Journaling is an incredibly powerful self-development tool that can support both our personal healing *and* our manifesting journeys. Giving ourselves the space to write freely can help us to unpack, process, and understand our thoughts, feelings, and emotions more clearly. There is also something immediately liberating about writing something down; it is as though the moment you release the thoughts from your mind and onto the paper, you change their vibration and the power they have over you, and in doing so you *let them go.*

✏ EXERCISE

This is a journaling exercise for you to follow, which I have designed specifically to:

- help you recognize your triggers
- identify where they stem from
- explore alternative ways you could have responded to the trigger to serve as a learning opportunity

Begin by thinking of an incident when you were triggered to feel low-vibrational emotions, such as sadness, fear, resentment, or anger.

1. Write down a detailed description of the trigger, *how it made you feel and what emotions it brought up for you.* E.g. I was having a conversation with my partner and they made a comment that made me feel like I was being rejected and I felt really sad, hurt, and upset.

....
....
....
....
....
....
....

2. Describe some other memories or experiences that you can remember making you feel that way.

....
....
....
....
....
....
....
....
....

3. Write down an alternative, more empowering way that you could have interpreted or responded to the initial trigger.

....
....
....
....

> You can replicate this exercise in a separate journal or notebook anytime you want to explore the source of your triggers and heal the wounds.

When you embark on your healing journey, it is not uncommon to find that you start remembering things you had previously forgotten, or that you start to experience flashbacks, some significant and some seemingly random. It's understandable that as you start processing the past, your subconscious begins to bring more memories into your conscious mind. For me this is a good sign, because these memories are resurfacing to be seen, healed, and let go. Don't ignore them, but instead see what they are trying to show or tell you.

Journaling is the perfect way to explore what these memories are trying to reveal. As you describe a memory include:

a) how you felt in that situation, b) what else was going on in your life at the time, and c) what consequences that event had on your emotional state, your feelings of self-worth, or your belief system. *While doing this, you may have an "aha" moment, as you suddenly realize how that experience, or that time of your life, has been influencing you ever since. You may also recognize certain patterns in your relationships or in your own behaviour.*

2. Inner-child meditation

This technique is one that helped me make what felt like cosmic shifts in my healing process. The first time I did an inner-child meditation was with my friend and healing coach Carina Talla. I reached out to her at a time when I was becoming increasingly aware of how challenging I found it to be vulnerable with the people in my life. I have always held this deep fear that if I was vulnerable in my relationships, then those people would abandon me. This wasn't just happening in romantic relationships but also in my friendships. I convinced myself that if I ever felt like I *needed* or *relied* on anyone for emotional support, they would sense that and it would drive them away. It's why I have often struggled with the idea of commitment or why I've trapped myself in cycles of getting close to people then distancing myself if I felt I was getting too "attached." If I hadn't heard from a friend for a week or two, I would panic and my inner voice would ask, *Do they not like me anymore? Did I do something wrong?* And I would either overcompensate by bombarding them with generosity or pull back from them as a form of self-preservation. Again, just as I had been triggered by the text conversation with my ex-boyfriend, I was allowing old experiences of rejection and unworthiness to inform the feelings of fear surrounding my current friendships.

I was determined to break the pattern and make a change. During my session with Carina, she held space for me to explore what kind of relationships I had formed in my earliest years and how they had impacted the beliefs I then formed about myself and my relationships with others. I had many memories from my childhood of feeling abandoned and dismissed, and, if I am totally honest, I was seldom given the space to feel emotionally safe, validated, held, or supported.

Identifying specific instances that had contributed to my patterns of thinking and behavior enabled me to reflect and compassionately say to myself, "Oh, well, of course I don't feel safe in relationships because I wasn't taught to feel safe within them growing up. *That makes sense now.*" That offered me instant relief and helped me to let go of that low-vibrational self-judgment, because at least now I had some understanding. Now I could see the wounds, not just the symptoms, and that meant that I could begin to heal and therefore break the patterns that were controlling the relationships in my life.

Carina encouraged me to think of specific experiences from my younger years when I first felt unsafe or rejected, and then she took me through an inner-child meditation where I used my mind's eye to take myself back to those memories. I replayed the memory and then I visualized my current self walking up to meet my younger self to embrace her, offer her unconditional love, support, and validation, and give her what she really needed at that time. As I did this, the tears started streaming, and they didn't stop for some time. I felt this magical feeling of love and compassion for my younger self and in this feeling of love I was releasing, letting go, and changing the power that those memories had unknowingly had over me. When I opened my eyes again, something had shifted.

WE CAN'T CHANGE THE PAST AND WE CAN'T CHANGE WHAT EXPERIENCES SHAPED US, BUT WE CAN CHANGE THE POWER THEY HAVE OVER US.

I take myself into this *inner-child* or *younger-self* meditation whenever I feel I need to process or heal something that is still impacting me. To do this, I enter into a relaxed meditative state by lying on my back and focusing on the rise and fall of my belly as I inhale and exhale, then I use my mind's eye to run through a memory that needs processing or healing. Then **I offer that version of myself the love that I really needed in that moment,** so I might tell my younger self she is safe, loved, validated, worthy, heard, and seen. Sometimes I do this for my inner child, but I also do it for experiences that impacted me in my teenage years or even much more recently.

Offering my younger self or inner child compassion has changed my life in ways I never expected. In truth, I had spent a long time avoiding looking back at my childhood. I just couldn't comprehend how focusing on the past could help empower my future. But I couldn't have been more wrong. Offering our inner child what they didn't receive at the time is integral to inner healing and our ability to manifest. It's integral because our inner child still lives within us all, and when we offer them the love, compassion, and support they always deserved *we heal.*

Carina Talla has created a powerful inner-child meditation to help guide you through this exercise, which is part of my collection of meditations and affirmation tracks that are available from my website, www.roxienafousi.com. Do not be surprised if you cry during these meditations; it is an emotional release, so don't try to hold back—*let it out and let it go.*

➡️ EXERCISE

After you've completed your meditation, I advise you to do this very simple and short journaling technique immediately afterward to really boost the healing effects of this practice.

Write down the answers to these questions after your meditation. Use the space here for the first one and then repeat the exercise in your own journal or notebook.

1. What was the memory?

....

....

....

....

....

....

....

....

....

2. How did your younger self feel at the time?

....

....

....

....

....
....
....
....
....

3. What kind words did you say to your younger self?

....
....
....
....
....
....
....
....
....

NB: inner-child work can be extremely triggering for some people and cause a great deal of distress when done alone. In this case I highly recommend doing this work with the support of a professional.

A NOTE ON INNER-CHILD WORK AND REPARENTING

Six months after I first started exploring the world of self-development, I remember thinking to myself, *That's it. I'm healed now.* I was in what I call **the self-help honeymoon**; the dark cloud had lifted and it was so exhilarating to see the light of life after living through a two-decade-long dark tunnel, and the high of that made me believe that I'd never be shaken, feel low, or face challenges again. It is a bit like when you first fall in love, and you think you'll never, ever have a single disagreement or argument with that person. It was naive, in hindsight, and now I know that healing is an on-going process that, like any relationship, takes work, commitment, and effort to navigate. But the further down the road you go, the easier it becomes to process and heal your wounds, and every time you do you enter a new chapter of your life and open yourself up to even more abundance.

For me a significant part of the healing journey is inner-child work and the commitment to *reparent* ourselves, to offer ourselves all the things we needed as children, such as to be heard, seen, validated, appreciated, and accepted. I have touched on it in the inner-child meditation exercise above, but there is so much more to inner-child work that can have incredible benefits for your self-development and manifesting journeys.

FEEL ALL THE FEELINGS

One of the reasons we can be so easily triggered by experiences from our past is because we didn't really process them when they happened. This is most likely because at the time, as young people, we weren't equipped to properly deal with them. Even as adults we have a tendency to resist any negative emotions that arise and instead try to escape from them. We use alcohol, shopping, social media, drugs, sex, and work to distract us so that we don't have to face our wounds. Unfortunately, though, this only serves to keep the emotional pain, and the low-vibrational energy that accompanies it, trapped within us. Think about it like this: if you had a lot of tension in your neck and shoulders, you wouldn't expect it to go away on its own, would you? You know that the longer you leave it, the worse it will get. So you find ways to release the tension and ease the muscles, such as getting a massage, reaching out to a specialist, such as chiropractor or a physio, or by doing stretches at home. We need to adopt the same mentality for our emotional body, working to release stored and suppressed low-vibrational emotions by finding ways that help us to move and let go of them. For example, by journaling, meditating, crying, talking to a friend/therapist, etc.

WE MUST GET INTO THE PRACTICE OF
EMOTIONAL EXPRESSION AND RELEASE,
ALLOWING OURSELVES SPACE TO TRULY
FEEL THE WHOLE SPECTRUM OF EMO-
TIONS SO THAT WE CAN PROCESS THEM,
LET THEM GO, AND, AS A RESULT, SHIFT
OUR ENERGETIC VIBRATION.

Consider for a moment in what ways you might be escaping
your own feelings. Can you identify when or how you do
this? It may be something obvious, like drinking alcohol
or distracting yourself with food, but sometimes we escape
our feelings in much more subtle ways. For example, I have
both friends and clients who are *constantly* overwhelmed,
exhausted, and busy. They keep taking on too much work,
or make themselves constantly available to meet the needs
of everybody in their lives, despite the negative impact it
has on their emotional and physical well-being. That can
also be a form of escape; we subconsciously make ourselves
as busy as possible so that we leave no room to be alone
and face ourselves.

I often think about why we are so accustomed to hiding,
denying, or escaping our feelings. Three reasons come to
mind: first, as children we are often told that crying and
expressing anger is "naughty" or "bad" and will be pun-
ished. I understand that boundaries are incredibly important
for children, but when we are told repeatedly that certain

emotions must be suppressed in order for us to be perceived as good boys/girls, it's no wonder that we become so adept at hiding them.

Second, difficult emotions are challenging to sit with; sometimes it just seems easier to have a couple of glasses of wine with your best friend than deal with the pain of your heartbreak. I spent a decade escaping with drugs and alcohol, so I completely understand this. But the easy route isn't the right one. **We need to feel, explore, and sit with our emotions so that we can process them; this is the path that will lead us to a greater sense of peace and contentment.**

The third reason that I believe we are so well practiced at escaping our emotions is because of the **toxic positivity** that exists within society. Toxic positivity is the obsession with remaining entirely positive, even during challenging times, and continuously focusing on the need to adopt a positive mindset. It encourages the dismissal of emotional expression for anything other than a positive emotion. It encourages us to adopt a facade of positivity even when we are in emotional pain or distress. Have you ever gone to a friend or family member and told them how you were feeling, only for them to say, "it could be worse," "just look on the bright side," or "it's not that bad"? I bet it didn't make you feel better. Even though the person saying this was most likely just trying to be helpful, it can make us feel dismissed, even silly—and *this is toxic positivity in action*. It stops us from feeling validated and then reinforces a subconscious belief that it is better to keep those low-vibrational emotions stored within us.

You might wonder how I can write a book on manifestation, which celebrates high-vibrational positivity, while condemning toxic positivity. It all comes down to the driving force of manifesting: **self-love**. It is not self-loving to deny ourselves the freedom of emotional expression. It is not self-loving to ignore or dismiss when things feel overwhelming or difficult. No, what *is* self-loving is this: giving yourself emotional validation and acceptance, committing to your healing journey, *and then* remaining hopeful and trusting that on the other side of the darker days there is growth and abundance. That is how you validate your low-vibe emotions without indulging in them. That is an act of self-love that will enable you to manifest even more powerfully.

CAN YOU REMEMBER A TIME WHEN YOU WERE HAVING A REALLY TOUGH DAY OR WEEK, AND THEN A FRIEND SAID, "ARE YOU OK?" AND YOU IMMEDIATELY BURST INTO TEARS? WHY DID THAT HAPPEN? BECAUSE THAT FRIEND OFFERED YOU THE TWO THINGS YOU NEEDED MOST: A SAFE SPACE AND COMPASSION. THAT IS WHAT YOU NEED TO OFFER YOURSELF.

When negative feelings and emotions arise, let them in, welcome them, accept them, do not judge them. Give them space to come up so that you can offer yourself the love and compassion you need in that moment to let them go.

For example, let's say you are on your social media and someone leaves an unkind message in your inbox. Instead of saying to yourself, "I know I shouldn't care. I know it doesn't matter," and brushing off any negative emotions that come up for you, try this:

1. Ask yourself how that made you feel. What emotions did it evoke?
2. Validate yourself by saying something like, "I feel sad, but of course I feel that way; it's never nice to hear someone saying unkind things."
3. Offer yourself compassion by saying something kind to yourself, by giving yourself the same advice you would offer your best friend, or by repeating a self-love mantra.

FEEL ALL THE FEELINGS SO THAT YOU CAN PROCESS THEM AND LET THEM GO.

FAQ:

Q: Does manifesting mean I need to be positive all the time? What if I have a bad day?

A: I couldn't even count how many times I have been asked this. It seems that many of you are putting yourselves under so much unnecessary pressure to feel good and "high-vibe" all the time, and panic that a bad day will throw you off course. It is driven by the toxic positivity I touched on above and the incorrect assumption that manifesting requires you to be happy and positive all the time for it to work. I want to make it absolutely clear to you now that this is not the case. Manifesting is a self-development practice to live by. That means it has to take into account the very normal highs and lows of life and the realities of what it is to be human. The expectation to feel constantly "happy" is a damaging one.

We are not robots; we are going to have days that challenge us, when we don't feel top of our game, and *that's OK*. I am someone that lives and breathes the seven steps of manifesting, but that does not mean that I don't get days where I feel low, anxious, stressed, or angry.

Giving ourselves permission to be human, to feel the full spectrum of emotions without judgment, to offer ourselves compassion, and to process what we need to let go of is what really matters. **It is that act of self-love that keeps you manifesting even on the days where being "positive" doesn't feel possible.**

Remember: we do not manifest what we think about; we manifest what we believe. It is only when we repeat a thought over and over for a long period of time that it becomes a belief. So if a negative thought comes into your mind, please don't worry that it means you will manifest it into existence.

Whenever anybody is blocked with their manifestation, I remind them of the most important lesson of manifesting: **we manifest from our subconscious beliefs about what we deserve and from our self-worth.** So if something you want to manifest is not showing up, you need to come back to this step and understand what fears and doubts are still blocking for you. *You have to commit to the inner work; there is no way around it.*

Here are some additional tools that I have found to be effective in removing fear and doubt that you can begin to use and incorporate straight away.

1. The past does not dictate the future

"What was and what is are different things."

REBECCA SOLNIT

When we think about things we want to manifest, our fear and doubt can take over and say things like "it won't happen," "you're going to fail," "don't even bother trying." Why? Probably because **our subconscious is trying to protect us from experiencing something that caused us pain or harm in the past.** It's not surprising when you consider that the primary function of the brain is to keep us safe. For example, if you were left totally and utterly heartbroken from a past relationship, your fear and doubt may try to protect you from feeling that way again by deterring you from meeting someone new or by encouraging you to self-sabotage your next relationship. Or if you went for an interview once and didn't get the job, your fear and doubt may try to tell you that you'll *never* get the job you really want and encourage you to instead apply for something that you're overqualified for and which doesn't offer you the recognition or pay that you actually deserve.

Remember, fear and doubt often mask themselves as friends trying to protect you from inevitable disappointment, when, in reality, they are actively holding you back from unlocking the abundance of the universe.

➡️ EXERCISE

Answer these questions to help you recognize when your past is getting in the way of your manifesting journey:

1. What is one thing you currently want to manifest? E.g. a healthy, loving relationship.

....

....

2. What is something that happened in your past that has made you doubt its possibility? E.g. my ex broke up with me and moved on with someone else really quickly.

....

....

3. What fear is that informing? E.g. that if I become invested in another person, I will be abandoned and rejected and left heartbroken again.

....

....

After you've done this, I want you to consider and remember something extremely important:

WHO YOU ARE NOW IS NOT WHO YOU WERE THEN. YOU HAVE CHANGED, GROWN, AND EXPANDED SINCE THAT TIME. YOU ARE CHANGING EVERY DAY. YOU ARE MORE RE-SILIENT, MORE AWARE, MORE SELF-LOVING, AND, WITH THE POWER OF MANIFESTATION BEHIND YOU, YOU HAVE THE POWER TO CHOOSE HOW THE NEXT CHAPTER PLAYS OUT. TRUST IN YOURSELF.

With that in mind, I want you to now continue this exercise by answering the following questions:

3. How have I grown since that time and what have I learned?

....
....
....
....
....
....
....
....

4. What could I do differently to ensure a different outcome?

....

....

....

....

....

....

....

....

There is a mantra that I love to use and which I would recommend repeating to yourself anytime you become aware of fear arising as a result of a past experience. The mantra is "**The past does not dictate my future**," Saying this to ourselves reminds us that just because something didn't work out before does not mean that it won't work out this time, or another time in the future.

Repeat after me: **the past does not dictate my future**.

2. Mindfulness

Mindfulness is a state of awareness. It's being mindful of the present moment and being fully immersed in the now, without attachment or judgment.

Mindfulness is a practice that transforms the way in which we experience the world. It can have profound effects on our well-being both on an emotional and physical level. For me it is the antidote to stress, overwhelm, and anxiety. It offers me the opportunity to practise awareness, gratitude, and self-love daily. It teaches me to immerse myself in the simple pleasures of day-to-day life, to stay grounded, and to ensure that I don't let life pass me by without *really living*. Most commonly people practice mindfulness through meditation or focused breathwork, but there are many other ways to practice it too; walking, exercising, listening, and even eating can all be done in a completely mindful way.

Mindfulness trains our brains to be more focused and provides us with more mental clarity, and therefore leads to an *increase* in productivity. I also find it helps me be more creative and innovative. When I practice mindfulness, *and shut out the "noise" of life*, I give myself the mental space needed for new ideas and perspectives to enter my mind. I think it's why I have all my best ideas when I'm working out or going for a long walk. On top of that, it is also a practice that can help us to combat fear and doubt.

Mindfulness can be particularly helpful when the inner critic, or the voice of worry, becomes overwhelmingly loud. You know, those times when the thoughts become compulsive or even obsessive, and it feels almost impossible to shut them off. They can start to have effects on our physical body too, making our stomach feel knotted, our heart rate faster, and our breathing shallower. It's a horrible feeling and at those times mindfulness is my go-to remedy. **Remember that you can only have one thought at a time**, which means that we can break the negative thought cycle by simply choosing to engage our focus and attention on something else. Engaging with the present moment is one of the simplest ways to do this; when you recognize that the voice of fear or doubt is trying to take over, choose one thing to focus on that is right in front of you and that can bring you to a state of mindful awareness. *You can use any of your five senses to help you focus into mindfulness.* For example, you can use your sense of sight to pay attention to what you can see ahead of you, focusing on the landscape or the room you are in, or you can use your sense of hearing to pay attention to any sounds and noises that you notice. As we bring ourselves back to the present, we instantly begin to feel more grounded as we break the cycle of thoughts.

"The present moment is the safest place you can be."
UNKNOWN

Here's an example of how you could use this day-to-day. Let's say you were at a dinner with a large group of friends and someone made a joke about you that *just didn't land right*. It hit something in you that triggered self-doubt. Immediately negative thoughts begin to creep in and, as they get louder, you start to feel your chest tighten. As soon as you notice what is happening, bring your attention back to the room, focusing on the details of what you can see, or listening carefully to all the different sounds you can hear. I like to pay attention to all the colors I can see, naming them as I go. Quite quickly you will notice a mental and physiological shift as you ground yourself back in the present and away from the narrative in your mind.

To get the most out of this mindfulness tool, so that we can quickly access it when fear and doubt begin to take over, we need to practice it *before we need it*. Someone once said to me, "Don't wait till you are having a panic attack to learn to meditate; learn to meditate so that if you have a panic attack you know what to do." And it makes total sense; we need to become so accustomed to these tools that we can use them effortlessly and easily when we need them.

▱ EXERCISE

I want you to try this mindfulness technique for yourself right now. Place this book beside you to begin.

- ○ Start by noticing how you feel, emotionally, mentally, and physically.
- ○ Set a timer for two minutes.
- ○ Sit with your spine straight, either on the floor

with your legs crossed or on a chair with your feet grounded on the floor.

○ Start the timer and name the colors you can see or notice the sounds, paying attention to slowing down your breath as you do so.

○ When the timer is up, notice how you feel now. You should have quickly felt an energetic shift and a grounding effect.

Repeat this practice once a day for the next seven days, adding a minute in time each day to get yourself used to the technique.

THE MORE OFTEN WE DISRUPT THE INNER CRITIC, *THE VOICE OF FEAR AND DOUBT,* THE LESS POWER IT WILL HAVE OVER US.

3. Worst-case scenario

This is a much-loved tool in my family and it's something Wade and I practice with each other all the time, after seeing it on the hit TV show *This is Us.* In the show, one of the couples, Randall and Beth, rapid-fire their worst-case scenarios and voice their deepest fears and doubts to one another, without judgment of themselves or each other. *They bring their fears to light.*

Wade and I started to try it ourselves whenever we began to feel anxious, worried, or apprehensive. If something was bothering us, we would ask ourselves what the worst-case scenario was and then voice it openly and honestly. Doing this felt like an instant relief, and I started sharing this technique with my clients straight away.

There are several reasons why I think the worst-case-scenario tool works so well. Firstly, when we feel anxious or worried there is almost always a subconscious *worst-case scenario* that is driving it. For example, if you feel anxious that you may have left your front door unlocked, the worst-case scenario that is driving that anxiety is that when you get home you will find your home ransacked and all your possessions gone. Or if you are worried that you didn't perform your best on an exam, your worst-case scenario may be that you fail, you don't get into the university you want to go to, and that you *never* find a job because of it. Only when we voice these worst-case scenarios are we able to recognize how unlikely or far-fetched most of them really are. Sometimes we also need to use this technique to let ourselves see the humor in it and make light of the ridiculousness of our worst-case scenarios. I often find myself laughing with Wade before I've even finished the sentence because I realize how absurd it is that my fear and doubt are trying to subconsciously tell me that just because someone didn't email me back I'm suddenly a failure whose career is going to end overnight.

The second gift of this technique is this: voicing our worst-case scenarios give us the chance to recognize that even *if things did go spectacularly wrong, **we would be able to handle it***; we would find a solution and it would all be OK. It is such a relief to know that we have a back-up plan no matter what.

Here's an example of when and how you might use this yourself. Let's say your boss emails you to say they would like to see you in the morning for a meeting in their office. Immediately after reading the email you feel panicked, anxious, and stressed. What is causing this reaction? It's not merely the thought of having a meeting, is it? No, it is probably the worst-case scenario that your subconscious is attaching to it. So bringing it to light is the first step. In this case, your worst-case scenario might be, "What if my boss tells me she wants to fire me, and then what if I can't get another job fast enough and I have to move back in with my parents?" After voicing this, you can question how realistic that worst-case scenario really is and remind yourself that even if you did get fired, you would survive it, you *would* find another job, and you would be OK.

✏️ EXERCISE

The next time you find yourself feeling stressed, anxious, or worried, answer these questions to guide you through the worst-case-scenario technique:

1. What has happened to make you feel uneasy?

....
....
....
....

2. What is the worst-case scenario?

....
....
....
....

3. Is this a likely outcome?

....
....

4. How would you deal with the situation should it happen?

....
....
....
....
....
....

We so often catastrophize and imagine the worst-possible outcomes, sometimes without even realizing it. Whenever I sense I am feeling suddenly stressed or anxious about something, I always ask myself these questions and feel an instant sense of relief. This tool can help you become more aware of that worst-case scenario that is being driven by fear and doubt. It also reminds you that you can handle anything life throws at you. **You are stronger and more resilient than you think.** The worst-case scenario probably won't happen, but even if it does, you will find a way through it.

ANTICIPATION IS WORSE THAN THE REALITY

Have you ever completely dreaded going to the dentist? You think about yourself lying there with bright lights over you and wearing that mouth guard that stretches your jaw in ways you didn't know were possible, while someone prods and pokes your teeth, shouting things like, "E1, D2, BACK MOLAR." The anticipation might cause you to spend the days, even weeks, leading up to the appointment with a lingering fear and anxiety. But when you are actually there, in the moment, lying on the chair, was it as bad as you imagined? Or was it just something a bit uncomfortable that you got through, completed, forgot about an hour later, and ultimately were thankful for in the end?

Worrying about the future only serves to rob us of the present moment, and living in a constant place of fear does nothing but hinder our manifesting abilities. We know from our own experiences that the anticipation or fear of something happening is nearly always worse than the actual reality, *and we need to repeatedly remind ourselves of this.*

Remember: in life we will always experience things that are stressful, overwhelming, and challenging, but *we always get through them* and come out the other side stronger and more resilient.

4. Let go: Full moon release ritual

Letting go is an integral part of the whole manifestation process. For abundance, love, happiness, and success to enter our lives, we must create space for them to do so. We create space by removing what no longer serves us or is no longer aligned with our highest self and future goals.

I mentioned earlier that our emotions are often stored within us until we process and release them. When these emotions are anger, resentment, fear, shame, or guilt, they keep us trapped in their low-vibrational frequency, which directly hinders our manifesting abilities. I was talking to my good friend Denise Byrne, and she encouraged me to try a full moon release ritual every month, a time when we are encouraged to release all that no longer serves us.

I loved this ritual so much that I wanted to include it here, because I think it is such a powerful way to reflect each month on what it is that no longer serves us, and to release the fear and doubt that are currently blocking our manifestations. Here's an extract from Denise, in her own words, that explains the ritual and the step-by-step process for you to try at home:

FULL MOON RELEASE RITUAL BY DENISE BYRNE

Having a release ritual is an essential part of manifesting. How can you maintain a magnetic energy if you don't actively release all that is holding you back and no longer serving you? If you've never done a release ritual before, I am excited for you because this is such a liberating and empowering experience.

You can do this anytime, but I always connect it to the full moon because, cosmically speaking, it's the time of the month when energy is at its height and then releases. The moon goes through many phases but it's when it's at its fullest, every 29.5 days, that we can harness the full extent of its power, giving you a wonderful opportunity to call in what you want and let go of what you don't. While new moons signal the start of the lunar cycle and are a key time for reflection, introspection, and fresh starts, full moons are an opportunity to shed what doesn't serve us and add intensity to our goals.

There's evidence to suggest the moon can impact everything from our moods, our sleeping patterns, and even our menstrual cycles. If you're in any doubt about the power of the moon, think of it this way: the moon controls the tides in every ocean around the world. If the moon can influence oceans, guess what? It can influence you and your energy too. The human body is 60 percent water, so it's little wonder that scientists believe we sleep less deeply during the full moon and can also experience an increase in bad moods and anxiety. Our daily lives can seem so far removed from the moon, but that doesn't mean we aren't affected by its superpowers.

Full moon magic: the benefits

1. Unblock your energy

The full moon is the perfect time for identifying your fears, worries, and anxieties and releasing them. Whether you realize that it's financial worries that have been holding you back or self-doubt that's keeping you down, full moons have a powerful cleansing energy and can help you *let it all go*. To put it very simply, a full moon ritual is a little like decluttering.

2. Supercharge your intentions and raise your vibration

Ever heard that what you put out into the world comes back to you multiplied? Well, that's especially true during the full moon. The full moon is a powerful amplifier. It picks up on your energy and multiplies it, whether that energy is good or bad, high or low, so when you set intentions during the full moon you're giving them more power to manifest. Being the powerful amplifier that it is, when you feel good the full moon keeps those good vibes coming.

Full moon ritual: how to

What you need: paper, pen, scissors, candle, matches, bowl of water.

Step 1

Take the time to review the things that are, in fact, holding you back. Perhaps it's something you haven't been able to stop thinking about that's constantly distracting you. Maybe it's a negative encounter with a person, a difficult situation, a niggling anxiety, limiting self-talk, or a bad habit. Ask yourself, *What's not working for me right now? What's blocking my energy?* Then cut the paper into lots of pieces, writing down one thing you want to let go of on each piece.

Step 2

Take the pieces of paper, one at a time, and reread what you've written out loud or in your head. These are the things that are currently holding you back. It is time to let them go. After reading each one, repeat the words "This no longer serves me and I let it go."

Step 3

Light the candle and, using its flame, *very carefully* set each piece of paper on fire and drop it into the bowl of water. Do this with the deep intention of releasing and letting go, and when you see the smoke it creates, visualize it as your fear and doubt floating away.

Step 4

Now that you've said goodbye to what is no longer serving you, it's time for the exciting part: welcoming the good stuff into that newly created space. Harnessing the powerful moon energy, sit down and ask yourself what would you like to manifest in the month ahead. Make a mini vision board!

Congratulations! You've just completed a full moon ritual. All that tough stuff that has been holding you back, dampening your good vibes, and draining your energy is now gone, and by setting new intentions you're paving the path for future success—all with the help of the very powerful and extremely potent full moon.

CAN I STILL MANIFEST IF THERE IS STILL FEAR AND DOUBT PRESENT AND UNHEALED?

The simple answer is yes. We all have years, even decades, of stored experiences that have contributed to our insecurities, low self-worth, and self-doubt, and this requires an **on-going** removal process. Our inner critic is still going to try to make itself heard, and there are still going to be days where we may feel overwhelmed by its presence, but that doesn't mean we can't manifest powerfully and effectively while we are still on that healing journey.

Earlier on I said that in the days before *MANIFEST* came out I had a lot of apprehension about it and a serious case of imposter syndrome. I thought I would share how I dealt with that fear and doubt so that it didn't interfere with my manifesting journey and vision-board goals and still went on to become a *Sunday Times* bestseller. (By the way, I still pinch myself every time I say that!)

I'll start with giving you a bit of the backstory: when I manifested the book deal for *MANIFEST: 7 Steps to Living Your Best Life* with my UK publisher, Penguin, I had just eight weeks to write it if I wanted to release it in January 2022, a date that I was set on. It was an extremely tight deadline, and only now do I understand how short a time that was to write a book. Ignorance was certainly bliss for me at that point; I had never written a book before, so I naively thought that because I enjoyed writing articles for publications and because English was always my favorite subject at school that writing a book would be a walk in the park. I had even done the math: "Well, it takes me about an hour to write one thousand words, so forty thousand words should be forty hours. *Easy!* Eight weeks is *plenty* of time." But when I began, I soon realized how out of my depth I was; it was nothing like writing an article. In fact, I'd say that writing a book is one of the most challenging things I've ever done in my life and there is no doubt that I was stepping well outside my comfort zone. Writing a book, for me, is like designing a house: you start with the foundations, then you keep changing, adding, removing, reworking, and, even by the end, it's hard to say it's exactly as you want it to be. You must come to terms with completely letting go of the idea of perfection, because you could keep editing a book forever.

On top of the mental challenge, I was experiencing a severe bout of imposter syndrome throughout the entire writing experience. Every day that I sat at my laptop my inner critic was trying to tell me that I wasn't a "real writer" and that I would never be able to write a noteworthy book. It was made worse because I have always loved self-help books—they have been a huge part of my own growth and I absolutely believe that one book can change your life. But this meant that I was constantly comparing myself to other writers that I admired and thought that my style of writing could never match up to theirs. *They were proper authors, and I was a fake*, was what I thought. I didn't even allow myself to read any other book during the writing period because I didn't want to torture myself with comparison. But I had one shot at writing *MANIFEST* and I'd be damned if I was going to let my insecurities mess it up for me or get in the way of my manifesting process, so I practiced what I preach.

I started by simply acknowledging the fears. I didn't try to suppress or deny them, but instead I allowed them to come out and then to actively and consciously *choose a better thought*. I would repeat mantras regularly throughout the day, such as *I am capable of anything I put my mind to*, and I kept refocusing my attention on gratitude, immersing myself in a feeling of appreciation that I even had the opportunity to write a book at all! Then I romanticized the writing sessions by playing music while I wrote in my pajamas at my kitchen table with large cups of coffee, imagining myself looking back at this as being a pivotal period of my life. And, above all, I trusted that my passion and authenticity would shine through the words I was writing. I had full faith that the book would find its way into the hands of those who needed to read it.

Once I submitted the book, I let it go. I wasn't going to engage in concerns over what I could have changed or what I could have written if I had more time. I surrendered it to the universe. Then, just days before its release, I decided to pick up the book and read it for the first time. I got five pages in and starting cringing. *What a pile of rubbish,* my inner critic said. Again I had to forcibly choose to disengage with those thoughts. I chose not to trust my own narrative, to remain clear in my vision, to dream big, and to not let fear or doubt influence what I put down on my vision board. I didn't eradicate my fear and doubt, but I worked through them using the tools that I've shared with you in this book and the last, and in doing so I was able to **transcend** them and remain empowered on my manifesting journey.

THERE WILL STILL BE TIMES WE DOUBT OURSELVES, WHEN OUR LIMITING BELIEFS OR INSECURITIES WANT TO MAKE THEMSELVES HEARD AND HOLD US BACK, BUT WITH CONSISTENCY AND A DEEP DESIRE TO POSITIVELY CHANGE THE WAY WE EXPERIENCE LIFE, WE CAN LIBERATE OURSELVES FROM THEM. PAY ATTENTION TO ALL THE SUBTLE, INSIDIOUS WAYS THAT FEAR AND DOUBT ARE INFLUENCING YOU. COMMIT TO HEALING THE WOUNDS AND REMOVING THEIR HOLD ON YOU. LITTLE BY LITTLE YOU WILL SEE YOURSELF FLOURISH, EXPAND, AND UNLOCK EVEN MORE ABUNDANCE IN YOUR LIFE.

The journey of inner healing, and of removing fear and doubt, is the greatest gift that manifesting has given me. I am no longer defined by my insecurities, and I no longer give my inner critic the power to influence how I behave, how I present myself to the world, or what I expect from my future. I give myself freedom to process my feelings, no matter how uncomfortable they might be, and I offer myself constant compassion. In doing so I am able to continue to manifest effortlessly and powerfully. I know you have the capability to do the same.

CULTIVATE AND PRACTICE SELF-LOVE

"Only make decisions that support your
self-image, self-esteem, and self-worth."

OPRAH WINFREY

OVERVIEW

○ Self-love is the driving force behind manifesting.

○ Self-love is not a step in and of itself, but it underpins every other step.

○ When we practice self-love, we show the universe what we believe we are worthy of receiving, which then determines what we will attract into our lives.

○ To me cultivating self-love really comes down to one thing: becoming aware of the choices we have and the decisions we make in each and every moment.

○ Always ask yourself, "Is there a more self-loving choice to make?"

○ The ultimate practice of self-love is perfectly balancing what you need today with what your future self needs tomorrow.

Self-love directly influences the way in which we experience and perceive the world around us, the way we behave, and how powerfully we manifest.

One question I often get asked is, "How can I be proactive in reaching my goals without constantly worrying about what everyone else will think?" It's something that most of us can relate to. How many times have you stopped yourself reaching out for help, changing jobs, posting something on social media, expressing yourself, or trying something new because you were afraid of being judged by other people? **We don't do the things we need to do to reach the next level because we are paralyzed by a fear of judgment.** We place so much emphasis on other people's opinions of us and we obsess over the need to be liked by everybody. We look to others to make us feel worthy, loved, and appreciated. We look for the approval of others by checking how many likes we get on social media, what feedback we get from our boss, or how many invites come through our door, *and we allow that to dictate how we feel about ourselves.*

I was speaking to someone at a dinner the other day, a content creator on social media, and she perfectly articulated just how influential other people's opinions can be for our own self-perception. She said, "Sometimes I will take a picture that I absolutely love. I think it's a really strong piece of content that I will have put a lot of effort into creating. Then I put it on Instagram and if it doesn't get many likes, I will look at the same picture that I loved thirty minutes ago and think, *Actually I really don't like it; it's total rubbish.*" We can totally distort our view of ourselves based on feedback from others, meaning that our self-worth is dependent on external sources. **We manifest what we believe we are worthy of, so if our self-worth is not built on a strong internal foundation but on the fleeting and ever-changing opinion of others, how can we powerfully and consistently attract abundance into our lives?**

HOW DO I STOP CONSTANTLY SEEKING EXTERNAL VALIDATION AND INSTEAD PRIORITIZE INTERNAL VALIDATION?

First we must understand where our need for external validation comes from. To me it makes complete sense that we have a deep need to seek approval from others. From our earliest years most of us are taught that to be *lovable* we must obey, listen to, and please our parents or guardians. Simultaneously we are told what, *and who*, not to be; we are conditioned to be what other people need us to be. We come to believe that love is not unconditional but absolutely *conditional*, e.g. "If you are a good boy/girl, then I will be proud of you and I will love you, but if you are bad, or you do something I don't approve of, I will be angry at you and I will take that love away from you."

As we grow up the same patterns continue; we seek approval from our teachers, our peers, our romantic partners, and, of course, society and culture. **We are constantly constructing an idea of who we think we should be in order to be lovable.** And that is the version of ourselves that we put out into the world, simultaneously losing sense of who we are and of our authentic selves. Is it any wonder then that so many of us base our self-worth on *external validation* and look to others to tell us we are doing a good job and that we are worthy? Or that it can feel uncomfortable to step beyond the norm when we are so conditioned to being agreeable to the people around us?

"We do not see things as they are, we see them as we are."

ANAÏS NIN

The thing about external validation is this, it's fragile, it provides a false sense of security, and it can be taken away from you at any point. This is because what other people think of you really has nothing to do with you at all. Our perceptions of other people, and other people's perceptions of us, are all dependent on a *culmination of internal factors*: the person's past experiences, memories, current emotional state, and their own view of themselves. So whether other people like you and approve of you is only a reflection of their own internal world. And the same goes if they dislike or disapprove of you.

With this in mind it seems reductive to focus so much of our energy and attention on trying to gain the approval of others, when, in fact, it has nothing to do with you and everything to do with them. To build our self-worth on a foundation that is stable, and that empowers our manifesting journey, we must instead prioritize **internal validation**. Internal validation requires us to validate, approve of, and love ourselves. It requires us to trust in our own decisions and base our self-worth on how we feel about ourselves.

When I started my career in self-development, I had to keep reminding myself to drown out the inner voice that kept questioning what people say or think about me. I knew that a lot of my peers saw me as a party girl, an addict, and I presumed they might not be very trusting or supportive of the "new me." I worked hard to ensure that my fears and concerns about what other people might think didn't interfere with how I showed up each day. For example, I made sure I never stopped posting about the things that mattered to me on social media (such as mental health and self-development), and I never shied away from being vulnerable or open about my own journey. I remained authentic in my message, and I knew that in doing so I would attract people that were on my vibe, and who would connect with me for who I really was, not who I was pretending to be. Since releasing my debut book, this has been even more important; as I share my message with a growing number of people, I am more open to criticism and judgment than I've ever been. I know that if I want to continue my pursuit to empower and inspire as many people as I possibly can, and to fulfill my purpose, then I have to be OK with the fact that not everyone is going to be on board with me, or my manifesting message. My self-worth must, therefore, come from internal validation.

Rather than constantly seeking the approval of others we must ask ourselves: do we like who we are? Do we approve of what we do? Do we respect ourselves? Are we proud of the way we showed up? Do we believe we are worthy of abundance?

DECISIONS, DECISIONS

How often do you look to other people to validate your choices? Do you find yourself constantly calling friends, a partner, or family members to help you make both the simplest and most important decisions in your life? *What should I eat tonight? What picture should I post? Do you think I should send this text? What should I say to my boss? What should I wear? Do you think I should leave my partner? Should I apply for this job?* Of course wanting the opinions of our closest friends is totally normal, but **it becomes problematic when we rely on them to dictate the choices we make.**

One way in which we can cultivate internal validation is to build **self-trust**. We do this by prioritizing our own opinions above others, becoming more comfortable in making our own decisions, and trusting our own intuition. I want to encourage you to become practiced at this so I have created a **short self-reflection template** for you to use when making decisions:

1. What are the choices presented to me?
2. What do I feel is the right choice?
3. Is this choice authentic to me?
4. Is this choice aligned with my future vision?
5. What is my reason for making this decision?
6. Do I approve of my own choice?

It is both liberating and empowering to be able to trust in, and value, our own decisions and choices without the constant need for approval or reassurance from others. The more we practice this, the more we begin to align ourselves with who we really are— with our authentic self. *We begin to live life on our own terms.* In doing this we cultivate self-love and boost our manifesting powers.

Switching external validation for internal validation

Whenever we seek validation from outside ourselves, we give away our power.

▱ EXERCISE

In this exercise I invite you to reflect on the areas where you currently find yourself seeking external validation. Then ask yourself how you can give yourself that validation instead. For example, if you are seeking to feel love from your partner, how can you give yourself that love? If you are always looking to make your parents proud, what could you do to make yourself feel proud? How can you give yourself the metaphorical pat on the back you are seeking?

1. Where am I currently seeking external validation?

....
....
....
....
....

2. How is this validation making me feel? (E.g. loved/ worthy/likeable)

....
....
....
....

3. How can I give that to myself?

....
....
....
....

THE NEED TO BE LIKED

"Stop trying to be liked by everyone;
you don't even like everyone."

UNKNOWN

As well as seeking external validation, many of us become obsessed with the need to be liked. We constantly monitor what we say and do to appease those around us. We play it safe and try to ensure we don't do anything that could lead to us being criticized or disliked. Quite frankly it's exhausting. It's exhausting because being liked by everyone is an impossible feat. There is no one on this earth who is universally liked. Not one single person. Just take a second to think about any celebrity or public figure; as many people as there are who love, adore, and admire them, there are those who dislike, judge, and criticize them for the very same things.

Finding peace with the fact that not everybody is going to love you is not only liberating; it is integral for us to align our behavior with our most authentic selves and the future version of ourselves that we most want to embody. This means that it is also vital for our manifesting journey. This is because energy is directional; you cannot focus your energy on your own goals and visions while simultaneously worrying if other people like you or not. Think about it: if you are constantly concerned with what other people think or might say, will you ever really take the risks and *do what you need to do* to expand your reality? No. As long as you are attached to the need to be liked, you will always be holding back *on a conscious and subconscious level,* and therefore you will always be limiting what you manifest into your life.

We all have to become OK with the fact that not everyone is going to like us. My mum used to say to me, "You can't please all the people all the time." She was right. So what I'm really trying to say is: *just be you.* Be who you want to be, focus on liking yourself, being proud of yourself, and being authentic to who you are and who you want to become. That is self-love.

➡ EXERCISE

Write down a list of at least twenty things that you like about you; they can be your qualities, traits, quirks, characteristics, passions, hobbies.

1 ....

2 ....

3 ....

4 ....

5 ....

6 ....

7 ....

8 ....

9 ....

10 ....

11 ....

12 ....

13 ....

14 ....

15 ....

16 ....

17 ....

18 ....

19 ....

20 ....

SELF-COMPASSION

When it comes to self-love, and how we can *really* cultivate it in our lives, there is one thing that I think is at the foundation: **self-compassion**. To me self-compassion means being soft and gentle with ourselves; it means nurturing

93

and mothering the inner child within us; it means being understanding of our needs; and it means giving ourselves space to feel, express, and process the full spectrum of our emotions. With self-compassion we relinquish the need to be "perfect" and instead accept ourselves as we are, embracing our magnificent uniqueness. Self-compassion creates a safe space for us to grow, step outside our comfort zone, and flourish into the greatest and most powerful version of ourselves that exists.

I spoke about the importance of self-forgiveness and non-judgment in *MANIFEST*, and self-compassion is fundamental in helping us practice this too. We all have times that we look back on and think, *Why did I do that?* We can answer that from a place of low-vibrational self-judgment or we can choose to use self-compassion to inform our answer. Self-compassion offers you the gentle and kind perspective that you need and deserve; whatever happened and whatever you did, you were doing what you thought was right at the time, and sometimes that was driven by pain, insecurity, or hurt. **Self-compassion says, I do not judge, I forgive.**

Think about it like this: if you were helping a child learn to ride a bike for the first time, what would you do if they fell over and then told you they were too afraid to try again? You would be compassionate, right? You would be gentle and patient, and you would encourage them to keep going. That kindness and compassion would encourage the child to try again, to learn and grow, and in doing so their confidence would build. And yet what do we do when we struggle, fail, or feel afraid? We berate, judge, and condemn ourselves. Imagine if instead we treated ourselves the way we would treat a young child, with love and kindness. Imagine how that would impact how often we pushed through our comfort zones, tried again, and gave ourselves the strength to grow and learn. Can you see, then, how self-compassion could so wonderfully influence how powerfully we manifest?

STOP BEING SO HARD ON YOURSELF

Where in your life are you being hard on yourself? Where are you constantly judging yourself? Do you permanently feel guilty about the way you parent, are you overly critical about the way you look, or do you put pressure on yourself to overachieve at work?

In the following exercise I want you to identify areas in your life where you are being too hard on yourself, and then find a way to offer yourself greater compassion. (Imagine you are talking to your best friend if this is difficult.) For example, if you are feeling constantly guilty about not having enough energy to be playful with your children after work, perhaps you could remind yourself that you go to work to support them, that you are doing your best, and that one person can only do so much.

▱ EXERCISE

1. Where I am hard on myself:

....
....
....
....

2. A compassionate message to yourself:

....
....
....
....
....
....

AS YOU PROGRESS ON YOUR MANIFEST-
ING AND INNER HEALING JOURNEYS,
MAKE COMPASSION THE DOMINANT EX-
PRESSION OF LOVE.

YOU ARE THE WHOLE PACKAGE

I had struggled with my confidence for as long as I could remember. I never, ever felt like I was enough. I constantly worried about what everyone else thought of me and I allowed my inner critic to stream an endless supply of insults. I remember turning to a friend of mine, Lily. She is someone who just oozes confidence and assuredness. She's unapologetically herself and unsurprisingly the first girl to support, cheerlead, and uplift all the other women around her; *she projects her own self-love onto others.* I have always admired Lily's confidence and one day I asked what her secret was. She said, "Roxie, you've got to zoom out and see yourself as the full package. Stop seeing yourself as the negative qualities you focus in on."

A penny dropped. **We so often see ourselves as all the things we are not, focusing our attention on where we feel we fall short, rather than directing our attention where it should be: on all the things that we already are.** I stepped back and began to see myself as a whole package. I am a mother, a friend, a daughter, a coach; I am someone that is always learning and growing, I am open and honest, I am self-aware, and I am someone that feels fulfilled when helping others. *I am many things.* **You are many things too.** You are so much more than the things your inner critic makes you focus on. You are the whole package! You have so much to offer the world and the people around you. The more attention you pay to what makes you so wonderfully unique, the more self-love you will cultivate and the more powerfully you will manifest.

▱ EXERCISE

Find your favorite picture of yourself and stick it in the middle of a piece of paper. Around the picture, I want you to write down any words or phrases that best describe you, so that at the end of the exercise the page will be a full picture of who you are and all the things you offer to the world.

Step 1. Find and print your favorite picture of yourself.

Step 2. Stick the picture in the middle of a sheet of card.

Step 3. Around the picture write down any words of phrases that best describe you, so that at the end of the exercise the page will be a full picture of who you are and all the things you offer to the world.

Step 4. Place the card somewhere you can see it to serve as a constant reminder of your magnificent uniqueness.

WHAT IF PEOPLE THINK I'M ARROGANT?

I find that, for women especially, one thing that really prevents us from being truly comfortable with feeling confident in ourselves is a fear of coming across as "arrogant." We favor self-deprecation over self-celebration, we bat away compliments, and we are overly cautious about not coming across as too self-assured. Culture and society have often stigmatized women who are confident, who aren't afraid of saying what they want, and who are unashamedly themselves. This contributes to a subconscious belief that being "too confident" will make us unlikeable. But here's what I want to remind you: being confident does not equate with being arrogant. You can be both confident and humble, kind and strong, direct and compassionate. In fact, the more confident we are in ourselves, the more we are able to inspire, celebrate, and lift others.

Let's change the narrative. Let's stop playing small to make others feel comfortable. Let's stop judging confidence as arrogance. Let's give ourselves and others permission to shine.

CULTIVATE AND PRACTICE SELF-LOVE

You deserve to love yourself. You deserve to feel worthy. As you go on this manifestation journey, allow self-love and self-compassion to override the inner critic that has plagued you for so long. Be vigilant with your thoughts. When the inner voice of self-loathing or self-judgment begins to speak, say to yourself, "**NO, we don't do this anymore,**" and choose something kind to say instead. Make a conscious and concerted effort to replace low-vibrational thoughts. Prioritize internal validation over external and remember that the most important opinion of you is your own. Remember: the more authentic we are, and the more we cultivate self-love in our lives, the more effortlessly we will manifest so that we can unlock the abundance of the universe.

RAISE YOUR VIBRATION IN TWO MINUTES

Complete the following sentences:

1. I am so grateful that . . .

. . . .

2. I am so proud that . . .

. . . .

3. I am inspired by . . .

. . . .

4. I am looking forward to . . .

. . . .

5. I really love . . .

. . . .

STEP 3
ALIGN YOUR BEHAVIOR

"Only when your intent and actions are in alignment can you create the reality you desire."

STEVE MARABOLI

OVERVIEW OF STEP 3

○ Aligning your behavior means showing the
universe, in action, what you believe you deserve,
because the way you behave is a direct reflection of
your self-worth.
○ Manifesting is not a passive experience; it requires
you to be proactive in attracting the things you
desire into your life.
○ Fake it till you become it and behave the way your
future self would.
○ Stepping outside your comfort zone is non-
negotiable on your manifesting journey.
○ Magic happens outside your comfort zone.
○ Align your behavior with your most authentic self
because authenticity is magnetic.
○ Create healthy habits that help you cultivate self-
love and embody the person you want to become.

A lot of people have said to me that one of their big-
gest takeaways from *MANIFEST* was the realization that
simply visualizing what you wanted to attract into your
life was not enough; manifesting **really requires you
to put in the work**, to make an effort and be proactive.

There is no substitute for hard work, commitment, and persistence.

Aligning your behavior is about understanding that *you are in constant dialogue with the universe.* You are always showing it, with everything you do, how worthy you believe that you are of receiving abundance. The way you treat yourself, the boundaries that you put in place, the respect you treat your body with, the relationships you give energy to, the way you spend your time, the habits and routines you commit to, *it all matters.*

To create change, you must *be the change.*

On our manifesting journeys we must ask ourselves, **"Where can I make a change within myself and the way I behave to create a change within my reality?"** It's also important to know that the changes we make don't have to be dramatic to be powerful catalysts for transformation. On the contrary, **it's often the subtle shifts that, when committed to consistently, create lasting and powerful change.**

Here are some exercises that could help you to clarify how to align your behavior and what shifts you can make to unleash the most empowered version of yourself.

➡ EXERCISE

The most important thing to ask yourself when you embark on any manifesting journey is, "Who do I want to become?" Thinking about this before you answer the following questions:

Start by visualizing **the person you want to become five years from now**. For the purpose of this exercise you don't need to think about the things you *want* or any particular goals you would like to have reached; I just want you to think about how this version of you feels, thinks, behaves, acts, and responds to the world around them.

Answer these questions from the perspective of your most empowered future self, so start each answer with "I am/I do."

1. How do you *feel* about yourself? What do you love most about the person that you have become? How lovingly do you speak to yourself?

....
....
....
....
....

2. What do you do to look after your mind and body?
   What does your day-to-day routine look like, and
   which healthy habits do you commit to daily?

....

....

....

....

....

3. How do you *feel* within the significant relationships
   in your life? How do you communicate your needs
   within these relationships and how do you respond
   to other people's needs?

....

....

....

....

....

4. What are some of the boundaries you set and
   honor? For example, what behaviors do you not
   accept from others, or what boundaries do you set
   to honor your work/life balance?

....

....

. . . .
. . . .

5. How do you show up at work? What characteristics
   and behaviors help you to be the best that you can
   be within your career?

. . . .
. . . .
. . . .
. . . .

6. How do you deal with challenges/obstacles and
   stress? Are there any specific techniques you use?

. . . .
. . . .
. . . .
. . . .

7. How do you feel and behave in social situations?
   How confidently do you present yourself to the
   world?

. . . .
. . . .
. . . .
. . . .

8. How easy do you find it to say how you feel/what you want and say no to the things that no longer serve you?

....
....
....
....

9. What behaviors/patterns/habits do you *no longer engage with* because you recognized they were not serving your highest self?

....
....
....
....
....

10. Do you commit time for rest/play/adventure?

....
....
....
....
....

Reflecting on those answers, I want you to think about where you are at currently. How many of those things are you not doing yet? And then ask yourself, *why not?* Why are you are not doing the things you know will empower you most? Is it out of fear? Is it because you've got stuck in a rut of doing what you've always done? Those things you've written down are all things you can begin to implement from this moment. In *MANIFEST*, I presented the concept of "fake it till you become it"—and this is precisely how you do that. *Step into the character of your future self*, begin to embody them this very second, until eventually you become them.

I want you to write down ten actionable changes you can make now to begin aligning your behavior with the future self you described above.

1 . . . .
2 . . . .
3 . . . .
4 . . . .
5 . . . .
6 . . . .
7 . . . .
8 . . . .
9 . . . .
10 . . . .

> If you are struggling to think of ten, why not join the MANIFEST WITH ROXIE Facebook group where you can get ideas?

Commitment letter

I commit to implementing the ten changes listed above because I recognize that to create change I must be the change. I commit to them because I am worthy and deserving of unlocking the most empowered version of myself that exists.

Signed ....

Date ....

BREAKING FREE FROM YOURSELF

So many of us get stuck in the comfort of the familiar. We stay stuck in relationships, jobs, and behavioral patterns that no longer serve us because we have got so used to them that we have allowed those things to define us. **When we define ourselves with anything, we risk being restricted by them.**

Here's a simple example to demonstrate my point. I have a friend who has always been late for absolutely everything. I'm sure you have a friend like that too, or maybe *you are that friend*. She would always say things like, "You know me, time management is not my thing," or "Always tell me that we're meeting earlier, so that when I'm late I'll really be on time," which is another way of saying, "This is who I am, so you should probably just change what you do so that you don't get so frustrated the next time I inevitably turn up late again." This friend had become so comfortable with the fact that she was always late that she had allowed it to become a part of what defined her and then **continued to behave in alignment with that version of herself.**

While being late all the time hadn't really bothered her before, it was beginning to negatively impact her life. She told me that her colleagues had started making snarky comments about her tardiness and that her boss had called her in and told her that it was no longer acceptable to arrive late to work and that she must, under no circumstances, continue this pattern of behavior. My friend also expressed that she often found herself overwhelmed because her lack of time management meant that she felt she was constantly rushing everywhere and was permanently stressed as a result.

I encouraged her to reflect on how long she had been describing herself as someone who is always late. As long as she could remember, she answered. I asked her if she had ever considered that she could change that. Never, she said. "I think it's just the way I am." I asked her to begin to just visualize what a more empowered version of herself might do to manage her time better and how it would feel to be less rushed day-to-day. I suggested that she become aware of her internal dialogue and refrain from using phrases such as, "I am always late/I am terrible with time management," and replace them with something like, "I am better at time management than I've ever been," or "I am so proud of my commitment to change." I then encouraged her to find actionable ways to implement a change, such as by settings alarms, clear time guidelines to follow, and spending time each morning to plan her travel times more carefully so she could properly assess when she needed to leave home or work. Over a short space of time, with consistent commitment, she finally let go of her self-proclaimed title as "the one who's always late."

It is so easy for us all to just carry on living the way we always have, doing the things we have always done, with nothing ever really changing. Only when we open ourselves up to the idea that there may be a different, more empowering way of doing things, can we really begin to take ownership of creating the change we want in our lives.

I spent decades trapped in the idea that I was someone who was destined to be unhappy. I didn't grow up being taught or shown how to be happy; on the contrary I was brought up seeing sadness, constant dissatisfaction, and unhappiness as the default way of living. Then, as I grew up, I became so used to my own low self-worth and inability to experience contentment and joy that I started to become attached to the idea that that was who I was. I defined myself by those things and by the things other people would say about me too: that I was lazy, miserable, and an addict. I allowed myself to indulge in the "that's just who I am" narrative and so I stayed that way, *defined and confined* by those beliefs, labels, and behaviors. I could excuse my actions because I held a belief that I was *just wired a certain way* and that meant there was no point even trying to change. It was only when I read the book *Feel the Fear and Do it Anyway* by Susan Jeffers that I realized I was responsible for keeping myself trapped in the cycle of unhappiness that I lived in, and that I was solely responsible for changing the narrative and writing my own story. Then, when I discovered manifesting and embarked on my inner healing journey, I had to first let go of those labels and ideas about who I was, and all the parts of myself that were no longer in alignment with my highest self, so that I could give myself permission to behave differently. In other words, I had to align my behavior with who I wanted to become.

> YOU DO NOT HAVE TO DEFINE YOURSELF
> BY THE PERSON YOU HAVE BEEN. LET GO
> OF THE PARTS OF YOU THAT NO LONGER
> SERVE YOU AND THAT ARE NO LONGER
> IN ALIGNMENT WITH THE HIGHEST, MOST
> EMPOWERED VERSION OF YOURSELF THAT
> EXISTS. GIVE YOURSELF THE FREEDOM TO
> TRANSFORM AND GROW SO THAT YOU CAN
> BE THE CHANGE YOU WANT TO CREATE IN
> YOUR LIFE.

▱ EXERCISE

I invite you now to reflect on all the parts of you, your behaviors, and your life, that are currently keeping you stuck. We cannot reach the next level while we remain trapped by those parts of us that are holding us back. Be as honest and open with yourself as possible while answering these questions:

1. What behavioral patterns are holding you back?

....
....
....
....
....
....

2. What relationships in your life no longer feel
   aligned with your highest self?

....
....
....
....
....
....

3. What labels/ideas have you held about yourself
   that no longer align with your future self?

....
....
....
....
....
....

4. Is there anything else in your life that you feel
   is representative of an old version of yourself
   and no longer feels aligned with who you want
   to be?

....
....
....
....
....
....
....

Over the coming weeks and months I encourage you to use
this information to propel change. *Use these answers to guide
you through a renewal and removal process.*

By completing this exercise, not only have you already
started the process of freeing yourself from the parts of you
and your life that are currently weighing you down, but
you are also gaining a greater understanding of your *authentic self.* Remember: authenticity is magnetic, and aligning
your behavior means being authentic to who you really
are and who you want to become.

Thirty daily rituals to align your behavior

Everything that we do, from the minute we wake up to the minute we go to sleep at night, is a reflection of our self-worth and therefore directly impacts what we manifest into our lives. This means that the things that we do *day-to-day* have a profound influence on our future.

Here is a list of thirty things you can do day-to-day to align your behavior with your highest self and empower your manifesting journey. Each day choose a selection of these to do.

1. Drink enough water
2. Make your bed
3. Take your vitamins
4. Eat nourishing food
5. Exercise
6. Get enough sleep
7. Watch something that makes you laugh
8. Cleanse or declutter your space
9. Watch the sunset
10. Call your best friend
11. Do something kind for somebody else
12. Write down five things you love about yourself
13. Practice gratitude
14. Have a candlelit bath
15. Rest when you need it
16. Say no to things you don't want to do

17. Plan your journey times
18. Express love or gratitude to somebody else
19. Play
20. Listen to music that makes you feel good
21. Get lost in a good book
22. Reflect on how far you have come
23. Meditate
24. Do something you've been putting off
25. Journal
26. Practice yoga or stretch your body
27. Dance
28. Repeat a mantra
29. Set your daily/weekly/monthly goals
30. Talk to yourself like you are your own best friend

STEPPING OUTSIDE YOUR COMFORT ZONE

On any manifesting journey you will be required to step outside your comfort zone; it is non-negotiable—you cannot create change if you continue to do what you have always done. In *MANIFEST* I explained the comfort-zone cycle and the way in which our subconscious mind attempts to keep us trapped within it. To summarize, our subconscious is constantly trying to keep us safe, and what is safe to the subconscious is *familiarity*. It doesn't recognize if what is familiar to you is good or bad; its only concern is that it feels comfortable. So when you make a change or do something different, your subconscious panics—*"This doesn't feel familiar"* or *"This feels uncomfortable"*—and will try to bring you back to what it knows; in other words it will trigger you to self-sabotage. For example, if you grew up feeling unsafe in relationships, then that becomes what feels familiar. As you grow up, you might subconsciously seek out relationships that mirror this feeling of unsafeness within them. Then if you found yourself in a healthy relationship, in which you felt truly supported, you might find yourself self-sabotaging the relationship, because the subconscious is trying to get you out of this unfamiliar situation.

To align our behavior with our manifestations, we must get into the habit of regularly stepping outside our comfort zone. I often think of it as a skill we have to master, and the more often you do it, the easier it becomes. Understanding the comfort-zone cycle is key; we can recognize that the discomfort is coming from a subconscious aversion to change, and instead of trying to run from it or give into it we can work through it. This is where the magic happens.

Stepping outside your comfort zone every day doesn't mean you have to go skydiving, face your fear of spiders, or run a marathon. I would argue that those extreme ways of stepping outside your comfort zone are more designed to *shock* you out of your comfort zone. What I am asking is that you step outside your comfort zone in ways that are applicable to day-to-day life. For example, you might try a new exercise class that encourages you to lose your inhibitions, maybe you cook a new recipe, ask a colleague out for lunch to nurture new friendships, or send an email to a potential client, pushing through the uncomfortable fear of rejection. **When you get used to the feeling of trying something new and pushing through your comfort zone,** it will become easier to seize and create new opportunities that will drive you closer to your manifestations.

⇨ EXERCISE

Seven-day challenge

I want you to challenge yourself to do at least one thing that pushes you past your comfort zone every day. It can be anything, but the main thing is to do something that makes you feel uncomfortable in order to serve your highest self. Make a note of each time you do this over the next week and write down how it made you feel afterward.

Day 1

1. How you stepped outside your comfort zone.

. . . .

2. How it made you feel.

. . . .

Day 2

1. How you stepped outside your comfort zone.

....

2. How it made you feel.

....

Day 3

1. How you stepped outside your comfort zone.

....

2. How it made you feel.

....

Day 4

1. How you stepped outside your comfort zone.

....

2. How it made you feel.

....

Day 5

1. How you stepped outside your comfort zone.

....

2. How it made you feel.

....

Day 6

1. How you stepped outside your comfort zone.

. . . .

2. How it made you feel.

. . . .

Day 7

1. How you stepped outside your comfort zone.

. . . .

2. How it made you feel.

. . . .

I know that the thought of stepping outside your comfort zone can be daunting and I know how easy and tempting it is to stay comfortable. But staying in our comfort zone robs us from really living. It robs us from experiencing wonderful new things, from exploring new opportunities, and from expanding our minds *and our realities*. To live a full life we must free ourselves from the subconscious desire to stay confined to what we are used to and give ourselves the chance to experience everything the world has to offer.

EXCUSES, EXCUSES

Excuses are a form of self-sabotage and an expression of our fear and doubt. Excuses often start like this: "I'm too busy, I'm not equipped enough, there's not enough time, I'm too old, I'm too young, it isn't possible for someone like me." They give power to the limiting beliefs and insecurities that drive them, and they deny us the opportunity to align our behavior with our manifestations.

One actionable way we can create change and drive ourselves closer to the things we desire is to recognize when we are making excuses and then to take action to override them. In doing so we help to uncover our fear and doubt and actively work to remove them, as we disprove their reasoning. In other words, every time you tell yourself that you can't do something (in the form of an excuse) and then you go ahead and do it anyway, you show yourself *and the universe* that you are more powerful than your fears and doubts.

⇨ EXERCISE

Answer the following questions to help you recognize, understand, and override the excuses you tell yourself.

ALIGN YOUR BEHAVIOR

125

What are the excuses you are making?

. . . .
. . . .
. . . .
. . . .

In what ways do these excuses hold you back?

. . . .
. . . .
. . . .
. . . .

What fears or doubts are really driving these excuses?

. . . .
. . . .
. . . .
. . . .

If you were to override these fears and doubts, what action
would you take?

. . . .
. . . .
. . . .

. . . .

What are the benefits of taking action?

....

....

....

....

**Now, are you going to do what needs to be done, or
are you going to continue to make excuses?**

YOU ARE ALREADY READY

We know that to get to where we want to go, we must step
outside our comfort zone. We must break the barriers that
are created by our fear and doubt, and we must take action.
**I believe that if you are reading this you already know
what you need to do.** You know what you need to do but
you have been telling yourself you aren't ready for it. You
might have been saying, *"I'll do it when . . . I'm more equipped/
I have more time/I'm more experienced/I'm more confident."*

But let me tell you a little secret: **you are already ready**.
You already have the power within you to do all the things
you are currently putting off. All you have to do is *feel the
fear and do it anyway*. Take action, be proactive, and make
your dreams happen.

➡ EXERCISE

On the next page, you will see a circle that represents your comfort zone—that's where you currently live. Round the outside of the comfort zone I want you to write down everything you know that you need to do to reach the next level and to grow, expand, and evolve into the person you want to be. Then, as you progress on your manifesting journey, come back to this page and tick them off when you have done them. When they are all done, I want you to reward yourself—**celebrate yourself for stepping outside your comfort zone!**

"Bite off more than you can chew . . . then keep chewing."

JOE DE SENA

MY COMFORT
ZONE

THINK, THEN DO

One thing I have been talking about in my workshops recently is a concept I have called "THINK, THEN DO." People had been asking me how to manifest multiple goals at once, and how to overcome the tendency to procrastinate (which, as discussed in *MANIFEST*, is driven by fear). I thought first about what I personally do to stay motivated and to really practice and embody this third step of the manifesting process. I realized my approach was quite simple really: *I think and then I do*. It's an integral part of the way I align my behavior with the highest and most self-loving version of myself that exists and it's something that I've trained myself to do.

When I think of something I must do, *I do it*. For example, if a bill comes through the door, I pay it. If a friend asks me to connect them with someone, I write the email immediately, so they don't have to ask me twice. I don't allow things to linger on my to-do list, causing me to feel anxious every time I look at it. I don't waste time procrastinating, waiting to be ready, or making excuses. I don't keep putting things off because *I know how good it will feel to get them done*. It feels like I've developed a "think then do" mental muscle that I have strengthened over time, which makes taking action feel effortless. It reminds me of a phrase I once heard: "**If you want something done, ask a busy person.**" When we get into the habit of taking action, it becomes second nature. To me it is also a form of self-love, because it is honoring my future self and setting myself up to feel good today and less overwhelmed tomorrow.

When I say that I trained myself to do this, I mean it. This behavior couldn't be more different from the person I used to be. I was always described as the "lazy one" in my family; I am the youngest of four children, my siblings are dedicated and inspirational NHS doctors, and both my parents are Iraqi immigrants who grew up in poverty and worked incredibly hard to build a life for us all here in the UK. I, on the other hand, lived via the "minimum effort, maximum effect" motto. It would take someone asking me to do something multiple times before I got it done, I always left things to the last minute, and everything I did was always done half-heartedly. I was directionless, unmotivated, and always making excuses, much to the frustration and disappointment of my parents. I'm telling you this because I honestly believe that if I can go from *that* to where I am now, so can you.

I challenge you to get into a "**THINK, THEN DO**" habit. **Get into the practice of taking immediate action without letting yourself talk your way out of it.** My top tip for doing this is to use your imagination to fast-forward in time to consider how you will feel having a) done the thing or b) not done the thing. Version A always feels better, and so it's always the right choice to make. **Remember that** the choices you make matter, and they show the universe, through action, how worthy you feel and what you believe you deserve.

⇛ EXERCISE

Seven-day action challenge

Over the next seven days become aware of when you have the opportunity to take action, or *think then do*. Then write it down here and note how you felt after doing it:

Day 1

The action

....
....

How you felt before doing it

....
....

How you felt after doing it

....
....

Day 2

The action

....
....

How you felt before doing it

....
....

How you felt after doing it

....
....

Day 3

The action

....
....

How you felt before doing it

....
....

How you felt after doing it

....
....

Day 4

The action

....
....

How you felt before doing it

....
....

How you felt after doing it

....
....

Day 5

The action

....
....

How you felt before doing it

....
....

How you felt after doing it

....
....

Day 6

The action

....
....

How you felt before doing it

....
....

How you felt after doing it

....
....

Day 7

The action

....
....

How you felt before doing it

....
....

How you felt after doing it

....
....

BEING ALONE

How often do you spend time alone? I mean, *really alone*; sitting on the sofa while scrolling through your phone, connecting with people on social media, or exchanging voice notes with your best friend on WhatsApp *do not count*. A lot of us rarely spend time in solitude, and that might be because the routine of our lives means we are constantly surrounded by our partner, families, colleagues, or friends. Or it might be because the idea of being alone without distraction feels so confronting, *or boring*, that we actively avoid it.

But finding time for solitude is integral to your manifesting journey. Solitude, *to be alone without distraction*, offers you the space you need to support all seven steps; you carve out a sacred space in which to create your vision board when you are alone, you need to be by yourself to have adequate space to process, reflect, and understand your fears and doubts, and learning to be content and at peace in your own company is one of the greatest demonstrations of self-love.

I recently took myself away to write this book on a solo trip to Greece for five days. I was a little apprehensive about traveling alone, but as soon as I arrived I felt this incredible sense of lightness. I had time to really consider where I was in my life, how far I had come, who I had become, and what still needed healing. I had space to journal, meditate, and discover a little bit more about my most authentic self. **I genuinely enjoyed my own company and that in itself felt so empowering.** I left the trip a different person; I let go of some old wounds that needed attention, and I felt clearer on where I was heading next. I realized that spending time in solitude was a profound experience.

I encourage you to look at ways that you can carve out time for solitude. It might be booking a solo trip, or perhaps it's scheduling in thirty-minute candlelit baths before bed, going for a long nature walk on the weekend, or finding time to have a "date day" with yourself when you take yourself to your favorite restaurant or try out a new gym class. The more you can begin to appreciate time by yourself, and the more comfortable you feel in your own presence, the more easily you will be able to connect to your magnetic authenticity.

Aligning your behavior requires you to step up and show up. If you want to manifest something into your life, it is up to you to make it happen. You must break past the boundaries of your comfort zone, you must get into the habit of taking action, you must let go of the parts of yourself that no longer serve you, and you must step into the character of your highest self until you become that person.

SUPPORT YOUR MANIFESTING JOURNEY

I have collaborated with The Head Plan to create beautiful self-development products that will help support your manifesting journey. They are all available to purchase from www.theheadplan.com.

1. The Journal

The Journal is a twelve-week program to self-love and empowerment. It is a journal like no other; imagine having me as your coach every day for twelve weeks. There are weekly self-reflection exercises, daily pages, and space for your positivity journal, weekly reviews, and more!

2. The Mantras

A deck of fifty-two mantra cards designed to raise your vibration. Simply shuffle the deck, pick a card, and repeat it to yourself five times.

3. MANIFEST—the Deck

A deck of fifty-two cards to give you daily inspiration and remind you of the key teachings from *MANIFEST*.

4. The Notebook

A blank notebook for you to use in any way you choose, and I think it would be a great space for you to replicate some of the exercises in this book!

STEP 4

OVERCOME TESTS
FROM THE UNIVERSE

"There is no passion to be found playing small—in settling for a life that is less than the one you are capable of living."

NELSON MANDELA

OVERVIEW OF STEP 4

- On any manifesting journey you will be presented with tests to overcome before you can progress further.
- They come into your life to test your self-worth and your trust in the manifesting process.
- Tests come in the form of obstacles, challenges, or people that ask you to settle for less than you deserve.
- When things don't go our way, we are given opportunity to show up for ourselves while building inner strength, resilience, and courage.
- When we overcome a test from the universe, we will be rewarded with abundance.

I always say that this is my favorite of the seven steps. It's my favorite because it is the part of manifesting that I feel has made the most significant impact on how I respond to the things that happen in my life that are beyond my control. Manifesting isn't a case of *once you learn to manifest then life will be perfect and you will be able to control and dictate exactly how everything is going to play out*. No, life still comes with its share of challenges, obstacles, stresses, rejections, and misdirections. But this step allows me to handle those things with resilience and strength, and therefore helps me to ride the waves of life with greater ease and fluidity. No matter what I face, or what challenges I may meet, this step has instilled in me that **after every rock bottom, after every storm and every low point, there is** *reward, abundance, and a leveling up*.

ROCK BOTTOMS AND LEVELING UP

When I look back at all the times when I hit rock bottom and, *believe me, I have had more than a few of them*, they have *always* been followed by a rebirth and a cosmic shift that propelled me into a new chapter of my life. Before I discovered manifesting, rock bottoms felt terrifying; they were always coupled with a complete lack of hope and a fear that I was going to be stuck in that place forever. They could send me into long periods of unease, deep sadness, and a rut that felt near impossible to escape from. Now, though, with the power of manifesting behind me, the way I cope with challenging times is totally different. I see these lulls in my life as nothing more than tests from the universe that I know I have the power to overcome. They don't scare me anymore; they excite me.

I'll give you a brief example. Back in November 2021 I found myself in a situation that was incredibly triggering and that brought up a lot of unprocessed pain and trauma. It was overwhelming and I deteriorated quite rapidly into a state of chronic self-loathing, extremely low mood, sadness, and anxiety. I was reminded of the fragility of our minds and our mental health. One week I was fine and the next I felt worse than I had in years. In the past this would have been the start of a cycle that could last months. This time, however, I had the practice of manifestation to help me. First I had coping tools that I now knew how to use. Through the process of removing fear and doubt, I have learned which techniques are most helpful to me during challenging times, such as using mantras, meditating, and journaling. Second I had full faith and trust in the universe that this would pass and that something incredible was on the other side. I knew that the pain was there to teach me something and to help me let go of the hold some old wounds still had over me. With that belief I was able to allow myself to really *feel* the pain and the emotions that were coming up and validate myself in my experience of them. This enabled me to process them rather than simply try to escape from them or hide them, which would only serve to keep me confined by them. During this time I met up with a friend, the inspirational founder of the FilterDrop movement, Sasha Pallari, and the moment I saw her, I burst into tears. She saw my pain and allowed me space to express it. She sent me a message later that day that said, *You might not realize it straight away but getting through this is unleashing another level of inner power. Something incredible is coming for you.* She was right; four weeks after that my book came out and I entered one of the most exciting chapters of my life to date. Through that pain, I cleared something that had been blocking me, and since then I have been more confident in the person that I am than I have ever been.

Overcoming tests from the universe means knowing that the down days and darker times offer us an incredible opportunity for healing, growth, and expansion. When you get through them, you will be rewarded and you will level up.

LEARNING TO SAY NO

Overcoming tests from the universe requires you to say no to what isn't worthy of you. But so many of us find saying NO both daunting and overwhelming. If someone asks us to go to their dinner party, we say yes because we don't want to offend them. If someone offers to pay us less than we know we are worth, we accept it because saying no to money feels so impossible to do. When our boss asks if we can take on another client, we say yes because we are scared that saying no will be perceived as incompetence. **Instead of saying no, we keep saying yes.**

How many times have you spent hours trying to come up with an excuse to get out of the very thing you said yes to, or just sitting and *wishing* you'd said no to begin with?

Saying yes when we want to say no causes a domino effect of stress that lowers our vibrations and robs us of our precious time and energy.

Why does saying no feel so difficult? Usually because it triggers either guilt or a fear of being disliked. This is why **cultivating self-love is so intrinsic to this step**. When somebody constantly feels guilty for saying no, it's because they lack self-worth; they still don't feel they deserve to put their own needs first.

I used to say yes to everything and everyone. I was so desperate for people to like me that anytime anyone asked me for a favor, or for help, I would say yes even when it would hinder me in some way. I was so afraid of losing someone's love or acceptance that I put their needs above mine, over and over again. Now **I am the queen of saying no**. I would go as far as to say that learning to say no is one of the most empowering things I've ever done for myself. My life is, without a doubt, better in every way because of it. I manage my time better and I am less stressed, and I don't have to waste time thinking of excuses to get out of something I said I would do. It has empowered my manifesting journey too, because every time I say no I show the universe how worthy and self-loving I am, and it rewards that.

We are so afraid of saying no to people and we convince ourselves that they will react with anger, frustration, or disappointment if we did. But, more often than not, when you do say no, people respect it and move on (*and if they don't, it really has nothing to do with you anyway*).

Recently I was speaking at a conference where I met a really inspiring woman that I'd been following on social media. She is a successful entrepreneur with two thriving beauty brands and a large following on social media. She emailed me the next day asking to collaborate on a project, and the inner child in me (the part of me that desperately wants to please and be liked by other women) wanted to say "yes, absolutely." I had to catch myself. I knew I didn't have time for another collaboration or to take on another project. I knew that even though I wanted to, and I was so flattered to have been asked, I had to say no. But I felt really apprehensive about declining. I was worried she would think I wasn't grateful to be asked, or that I was rude, or that she would then disregard me. I had to sit with that, and then decided to serve my higher self, to overcome this test from the universe, and to say no. I had to say no so I could preserve my time and energy. I emailed back and told her the truth, that I would love to but I just don't have the time. She replied a few minutes later. There was no sign of her thinking I was rude or disregarding me, as my own fears had anticipated. On the contrary, she was nothing but kind and *completely* respectful of my decision.

Get into the practice of saying no, even when it feels uncomfortable. In doing so you honor who you are

and who you want to become. You send a message to the universe that says, "I know what I am worth, and I respect who I am." The universe will respond to that by bringing you things that match that high-vibrational frequency of self-love.

STOP SETTLING

I made a decision before starting *MANIFEST* that I would not swear in any of my writing, but I'm breaking my own rule here, and only here, because I really need to emphasize this point: PLEASE STOP F*CKING SETTLING.

So many of us are settling. We settle in our relationships, in our jobs, and in what we expect from life. We get so used to just "getting on with things" and we accept the old idea that "*life is hard and you just have to make the best of it*." We settle because we don't really believe we are worthy of more. We settle because we doubt the possibility of attracting something better. And by settling we send a direct message to the universe that we don't expect more, and so we don't attract more into our lives. **To overcome tests from the universe we must overcome our tendency to settle.**

➡ EXERCISE

To stop settling we must first understand where we have settled in the past, where we are currently settling, and, more important, **why we settle**. I invite you here to identify times in your life, both in the past or the present, when you have settled or are settling for less than you deserve. After you have listed them, ask yourself, "Why did I settle?" What limiting belief was holding you back? What insecurity was taking hold? Write the answers in the column beside it. For example, I settled with that friendship because I didn't really believe that I was worthy of respect.

I ask that you do this completely free of self-judgment and instead offer yourself compassion: compassion for the parts of you that did not, or do not, feel that you deserve more. By identifying when and why we have settled, we empower ourselves to make a change and choose differently next time.

I can't stress this enough: you will never make space for un-limited abundance to enter your life while you are settling for less than you deserve. I promise you that, no matter what, you **do** deserve the best. You do deserve to live a life that makes you happy.

WHEN I SETTLED	WHY I SETTLED

LET IT GO

Letting go is a constant theme that runs through the manifestation process. We have to let go of who we were, let go of what no longer serves us, and let go of limiting beliefs. Letting go is, to me, an act of self-love. It's making a decision that is not always easy for the sake of our future. But to let go we need **acceptance.**

Accepting something is over, not working, or no longer serving us is an essential part of letting go. Because when we don't we are simply trying to force something that doesn't fit and desperately trying to make something feel right when it just doesn't. **To accept something isn't working is to liberate yourself from what's holding you back.**

HEARTBREAK

For anyone reading this who is struggling with the ending of a relationship, or who knows they are in a relationship that isn't right for them, this is my advice to you: I know that endings are hard. I know that saying goodbye is painful. I *really* do know. I promise you this, though, *heartbreak will be the making of you.* I don't think anyone ever grows, expands, or changes more as a person than they do through the pain of heartbreak.

Accept the end and allow yourself time and space to heal. Feel all the feelings; cry, scream, let it out. Know that it is OK to miss them, but just because you miss them doesn't mean they are the right person for you. Trust that better days are coming, this too shall pass, and that you will experience love again.

Don't waste your precious energy on resentment or anger; every relationship serves to teach us and help us become who we are meant to be. Take time to reflect on all the beautiful experiences you had together, memories that will last a lifetime, and take time to consider all the lessons you learned. You are stronger than you think, you *are* worthy of unconditional love, and you are enough.

Sometimes things just no longer fit together. It's not personal; it's just the way it is—try not to attach more meaning to it than that. Take a deep breath, meditate, go for walks, watch movies, listen to music, practice yoga, work out, eat nourishing food, get a haircut, go for dinner with friends, book a holiday. Do nice things; be the love that you need in your life. It's all going to be OK, trust me.

I have reiterated the importance of letting go within the manifestation process throughout this book and the last, but I know that there can still be a lot of resistance around it. I think one of the reasons people stop themselves from letting go, and why they keep settling or stay stuck in certain situations, is because we often mistake letting go for "giving up." It can feel daunting to say that this thing that I started didn't work out, and I have to accept that and let it go. It can cause us to feel like we've failed or fear that we will be judged by others as a failure.

In my manifesting workshop in January 2022, there was a lovely lady in the audience who spoke up during the Q & A section. She said, "I opened a children's clothing store before the pandemic, and I have three children, and the lockdown hit us hard." Tears began to run down her cheeks at this point and then she continued. "I needed to take the store online and I know I need to close the shop. I can't do it all anymore; between the children and the store and the online shop, I feel like I am breaking. But I am so afraid to make the decision to close shop because I feel like I've failed, and I feel so embarrassed." The entire room of 380 people were thinking exactly what I was. *My goodness, you have done anything but fail and you have absolutely nothing to feel embarrassed about.* I hugged her tightly and I told her what she needed to hear, the truth. She hadn't failed; she was making an empowered decision to let go of what was holding her back. She was saving herself from further stress and pain. She was giving herself back the precious gifts of time and energy so that she could be with her children and focus on growing the online store. When she looked at me you could see the relief in her face. She smiled and whispered, "Thank you so much," and I could literally feel the weight being lifted from her. It was a beautiful moment that was felt by everyone in the room. Sometimes we need someone else to give us permission to let go and to remind us that we haven't failed. But, more important, we need to give ourselves permission to do that.

ACCEPTING THAT SOMETHING ISN'T WORK-ING IS NOT A FAILURE—*IT IS A POWER MOVE.* IT IS A RELEASE OF WHAT NO LON-GER SERVES YOU, AND AN UNLOCKING OF A NEW BEGINNING.

REDEFINING CHALLENGES

The greatest gift that this step offers you is to help you reframe every single challenge, rejection, or obstacle that comes your way.

The meanings we attach to anything and everything are what ultimately define our experience of the world. Often when something doesn't go to plan, or when we are met with adversity, we take it personally. We allow it to validate our insecurities or limiting beliefs. If someone ghosts us after a date, we see it as proof that *we aren't enough*. If our flight gets canceled, we say, "Typical, this always happens to me. I have the worst luck." If we lose out on a promotion to somebody else, we determine that we will never get to where we want to go.

I think this is especially important when we are faced with rejection. Rejection can be so deeply triggering. It can be really painful when someone essentially says, "I don't choose you." It is so difficult in those moments not to take it personally or see it as a reflection of how lovable, worthy, desirable, or likeable we are. Rejection can rock the foundations we stand upon and leave us feeling fragile, hurt, and vulnerable. It is at these times that we really need to show up for ourselves and offer ourselves the unconditional love, support, and compassion that we deserve. We need to remind ourselves that **rejection is redirection.**

Whatever challenge or obstacle we face, there is always a more empowering perspective we can take or a different meaning we can attach to it. We can choose to see it as an opportunity to teach us something about ourselves, to lead us somewhere new, or to help us push past our comfort zones.

➡ EXERCISE

There will be plenty of times in your life when you felt like things were going "wrong" but then it turned out to be for the best. Write down five times when this has happened. For example, you might have made an offer on a house that got rejected, which was a blessing in disguise because you love the house you eventually moved into. Or maybe you got fired from a job but it turned out to be for the best because it led you to set up as a freelancer.

1. What went wrong

....
....

    Why it turned out for the best

....
....
....
....

2. What went wrong

....
....

Why it turned out for the best

....
....
....
....

3. What went wrong

....
....

Why it turned out for the best

....
....
....
....

4. What went wrong

....
....

Why it turned out for the best

....
....
....
....

5. What went wrong

....
....

Why it turned out for the best

....
....
....
....

Use these examples to serve as proof that there is always a positive outcome to negative experiences. Remind yourself of that the next time you are faced with a test. Just because you can't yet see why it's happening, always know that there is a reason.

The test diary

I said in *MANIFEST* that on every manifesting journey you will be presented with tests that you need to overcome. These tests come from the universe to ask how worthy you really believe you are of having the things that you desire. *In other words, they test your self-worth.* Here is a "test diary" for you to use when you are next presented with a test to **help you make the most empowered decision possible.**

TEST DIARY

What is it that you really want?

What is the test you've been presented with?

How does it differ from what you originally put on your vision board?

If you accepted the test, what would you have to sacrifice?

What fear is influencing your apprehension around overcoming the test?

What would the most empowered and confident version of yourself do?

With that in mind, what are you going to do now?

Repeat this exercise in your own journals or notebooks whenever you need help with overcoming a test from the universe.

Every time you overcome a test you make a decision that is in alignment with your future self, and you say no to what isn't right for you, *you step into your power.* Stepping into your power is what manifestation is all about. You have the power to be whoever you want to be, and you have limitless potential within you. All you need to do is *unleash it.*

ENERGY PROTECTION

There are people and situations in our lives that fuel our energy; they make us feel good, energized, vibrant. They make us feel respected, valued, and appreciated for who we are. They support us on our manifesting journeys because being around those people, or in those situations, fuels those high-vibrational feelings of love, joy, contentment, enthusiasm, and passion. They ignite a spark within us that encourages and motivates us to keep moving forward and to flourish in our authenticity.

Then there are people and situations that drain our energy. They leave us feeling devalued, deflated, and unappreciated. They make it feel uneasy and uncomfortable to be ourselves. The energy we give out may be taken for granted or abused. They lower our vibration and hinder our manifesting journeys.

Protecting our energy is an act of self-love. Our energy is sacred, and we must honor it as such. We need to become aware of who and what drains our energy (*energy-takers*) and fuels our energy (*energy-givers*), then we must begin to set *boundaries*. Examples of boundaries are: saying no to what isn't right for you; communicating your needs more clearly to others; being mindful of who you spend time with and of your personal space.

FAQ:

Q: What if I have a family member who is an energy-taker? How can I set a boundary with them without feeling like I am abandoning them?

A: I understand that with family members setting boundaries can feel challenging. It's not as simple as saying, "Just remove yourself from the relationship and don't see them again." Family dynamics are complex, and we can want to distance ourselves from people while simultaneously loving them and wanting them in our lives in some capacity. My advice is to set boundaries that feel manageable and which honor your emotional state and mental health.

To do this you need to understand what frequency of contact feels OK for you, and *when* being around these people feels most manageable. For example, you may need to cut back on the contact or amount of time you see them, but not cut it out completely, and you may realize that you are best equipped to see them or speak to them when you are feeling at your emotional best; when you are feeling mentally strong you are less likely to be affected by their negative comments or their energy than if you were already feeling low, overwhelmed, on edge, or just tired.

To me this is how we can set and honor boundaries that ensure we put our own emotional and mental health first, but in a way that still feels manageable.

⇛ EXERCISE

I want you to reflect on all areas of your life and write down everything that fuels your energy in the Energy-Givers column; this can be a person, activity, self-care ritual, or place. Then, in the Energy-Takers column, write down everything that drains your energy.

After you have done this, I want you to think of five healthy boundaries that you can set and implement to help you protect your energy. For example, "I will stop saying yes to seeing my friend for dinner every Friday night, when I know that what I need on those evenings is to rest after a busy week at work," or "I will understand that I cannot be constantly available for my friend because I am not solely

responsible for somebody else's emotional needs." Write
them here:

ENERGY-GIVERS	ENERGY-TAKERS

FIVE HEALTHY BOUNDARIES

....

....

....

....

....

There are some circumstances when we find ourselves un-
able to step away from the people or things that drain our
energy. For example, we may go to work every day in an

environment where we are surrounded by colleagues or a boss whose energy feels toxic. They might be constantly complaining, or their energy may make you feel uneasy but you can't pinpoint exactly why; we can absolutely sense other people's energy, and so it's not uncommon to feel that somebody or something is an energy-taker without being able to give a precise reason for it. So how do we deal with these situations? How do we still protect our energy when it seems unavoidable to be around these people? I have two tips for you:

1) Be an observer

Remember: we have the power to choose what we allow in and what we focus our attention on. When somebody says things that are negative, rude, or low-vibe, make a choice to hear it, observe it, and then **let it go.** See yourself as the observer, without allowing yourself to get lost in *their* story and narrative.

You can use this anytime. For example, let's say you are in a queue. The person behind you is getting irate, frustrated, muttering under their breath, or talking loudly on the phone expressing their annoyance. You have a choice: you can join in their frustration, you can get frustrated at their frustration, or you can observe this person and then let it go.

2) Shake it off

After being in the company of someone that you feel has drained your energy, find a way to shake it off. For example, go to a yoga class, put high-vibe music on in the car on the drive home, practice a five-minute letting-go meditation, repeat a mantra, such as "I let go of the day and focus my attention on the present," or call your best friend for a catch-up.

"Energy doesn't lie. Trust the vibes you get."

UNKNOWN

WE CAN'T CONTROL WHAT OTHER PEOPLE DO OR SAY OR HOW THEY CHOOSE TO EXPERIENCE THE WORLD, BUT WE CAN CONTROL HOW WE RESPOND TO IT, WHAT WE ALLOW IN, AND WHAT BOUNDARIES WE SET. AS YOU EMBARK ON YOUR MANIFESTING JOURNEY, YOU WILL BECOME MORE SENSITIVE TO WHAT FEELS GOOD AND WHAT DOESN'T. PAY ATTENTION TO HOW THINGS MAKE YOU INSTINCTIVELY FEEL AND DON'T FORGET TO PROTECT YOUR ENERGY.

STEP 5

EMBRACE GRATITUDE
(WITHOUT CAVEATS)

"It is not happiness that brings us gratitude; it is gratitude that brings us happiness."

UNKNOWN

OVERVIEW OF STEP 5

- Gratitude is a feeling of appreciation.
- We can use gratitude to pull us out of a low-vibe mood.
- The manifesting sweet spot is knowing where you want to go, while being entirely grateful for all that you already have.
- Where attention goes, energy flows. The more you focus on the good, the more good will come to you.
- A positivity journal is a powerful tool to help retrain your brain to cultivate an attitude of gratitude.
- Switch "I have to do it" for "I get to do it."
- A grateful heart is a magnet for miracles.

When I was younger, my mum used to say a phrase to me in Arabic that literally translates as "For every thanks you give, you get a thousand in return." I also heard her whisper *alhamdulillah* (*thanks be to God*) countless times a day, as it was core to her religion of Islam. In fact, all religions place emphasis on the importance of gratitude. Science too has proven how powerful the effects of gratitude are for our well-being and physiology. Various studies have shown that gratitude helps improve sleep quality, strengthens our immune system, regulates stress, reduces pain, and improves the symptoms of anxiety and depression. The UCLA Mindfulness Awareness Research Center has shown that gratitude *changes the neural structure of the brain* and leads to greater feelings of happiness and contentment.

Gratitude is one of the most high-vibrational emotions we can experience. When we are in a deep state of gratitude, we become magnetic and we effortlessly attract more abundance into our lives. Manifesting is not just about focusing our attention on what we want more of; it's about appreciating all that we already have.

SLOW-DRIP DOPAMINE

I grew up, for the most part, void of joy, contentment, or happiness as I know it today. I hated being alone, being "bored" literally terrified me, and I tried everything I could to keep my pain bottled deep down within me. I escaped my feelings by chain-smoking over twenty cigarettes a day, binge drinking, and taking drugs. The only time I experienced happiness was when it came in the form of an extreme high, whether that was a passionate encounter with someone I was attracted to, going to an extravagant party, or being intoxicated. When I looked in the mirror, I saw a monster looking back at me. I would tell myself I was disgusting, ugly, revolting, and I wholeheartedly believed that for years. The only thing that would help me see something different, to feel an ounce of confidence, was cocaine. So rather than healing the wound of self-loathing, I got into the habit of taking my first line at 4 p.m. to give me a sense of "false confidence." My life was on a pendulum that swung between chemically induced highs and debilitatingly painful lows. There was no in between.

When I first met Wade in 2018 I was still in the grips of my addiction and secretly taking drugs in the bathroom on our dates. He, on the other hand, had never taken drugs, never drank to excess, and didn't smoke. He had something I thought was an impossible thing to possess: an ability to master moderation and balance. I saw something in him I wanted for myself; he was able to appreciate the small things in life. He found genuine joy in things like walking through a park, petting a dog that passed him on the street, and playing board games. I was, quite frankly, baffled by this. *How on earth was he experiencing so much happiness over such seemingly insignificant things, and how was he enjoying going out for dinner or staying out late in a bar without being high on drugs?*

While Wade and I were falling in love, we would stay up for hours talking about everything and anything. We talked at length about our pasts, our fears, happiness, life's purpose, meditation, and about my addiction. Wade held space for me to explore it safely; he never passed judgment or made me feel unworthy or ashamed because of it. I had just begun my own manifesting journey and, coupled with that magical falling-in-love feeling, I felt ready and motivated to make a change. I decided (*albeit not for the first time*) to give up drugs and alcohol. I went cold turkey and after a month had passed, which was the longest I'd been totally clean for almost a decade, something incredible happened; I was sitting on my bed talking to my sister on the phone, and I don't remember what it was about now, but I suddenly started laughing. Like, *really laughing*. You know that kind of belly laugh where you feel it in your whole body? It was an expression of genuine joy. It was such a foreign feeling to me that I still remember it as clear as day four years later.

Over the coming weeks this feeling came up more and more. I would be at breakfast, the sun shining as I ate my avocado on toast, and I felt . . . *happy*. Not drug-induced happy, not passionate-lust happy, just happy. I could only describe it as childlike joy. It was simple. I started to wonder, if my highs were constantly being created by chemicals or high-adrenaline events, was I setting the bar for happiness so impossibly high that perhaps that was why the simpler joys had felt incomparable and insignificant to me?

Wade and I started talking about my new way of living, and we jokingly concluded that instead of the extremes I had been experiencing before, where the super high would always be followed by an extreme low, I was now giving myself what we called "slow-drip dopamine"—a term Wade and I coined to describe creating **a constant flow of simple reasons to feel good**. Dopamine is a type of neurotransmitter and hormone that gives us a feeling of pleasure, reward, and motivation. It's well known that drugs can give you a big, fast increase in dopamine in your brain but you pay for it afterward, because the artificial high makes your body less able to produce dopamine naturally. But I started wondering what would happen if I could get natural highs from healthy, nourishing, and sustainable things that enriched my life rather than made me suffer? And what if— instead of using all my dopamine up at once—I could spread it out? I started to use that made-up term as a way of describing my future goals; *I wanted to live a slow-drip-dopamine life*. I started to focus my attention on the simple joys that come from innocent playfulness, nature, and expressions of love. **I began redefining joy and it was life-changing**. At the heart of it was making a conscious effort to practice gratitude and immerse myself in a state of appreciation for life's simplest pleasures.

Now the things that bring me joy are not found at the bottom of a tequila shot but in the things I used to perceive as mundane and insignificant. Now I experience true, genuine happiness and joy pushing my son on the swing, sitting on the grass, reading a book, making breakfast, being on my sofa, drinking coffee, people watching through the window of a cafe, being still, exercising, and cooking.

I think that many of us seek constant stimulation to make us feel good, happy, and joyful. We are in a culture where instant gratification is always available to us, whether that's via online shopping, our social media channels, dating apps, drinking, or sex. We almost condition ourselves to only experience positive feelings in these moments. We can rob ourselves of the opportunity to find pleasure in the small, simple, slow, subtle moments. The slow-drip-dopamine concept helped serve as a reminder for me to shift my attention and redefine happiness, and I hope it might do the same for you too.

In *MANIFEST* I suggested some techniques to help you cultivate an attitude of gratitude, such as making daily gratitude lists and completing a positivity journal every evening. Here I want to present a couple more gratitude practices for you to deepen your sense of appreciation, not just for the things in your life, but for the person that you are and the life you have lived.

I AM PROUD OF HOW FAR I HAVE COME

All too often we are so busy focusing on what we want from our future that we lose sight of how far we have come and all that we have already achieved. I love the quote "Remember the time when you wished for the things you have now?"—it is such a powerful reminder to stop and look at all the things we have manifested into our lives *already*.

▱ EXERCISE

I have created a guideline for you to explore and reflect on how far you have come and to show yourself the appreciation you deserve. Take your time on this exercise—light some candles, play some meditative music, and be as thorough as you can in your answers.

1. What adversity or challenges have you overcome to get to where you are today?

....
....
....
....
....
....
....
....
....
....
....
....

2. When did you make the best of a difficult
   situation?

....
....
....
....
....
....
....
....
....
....

3. When did you push yourself out of your comfort
   zone? When did you feel most proud?

....
....
....
....
....
....
....
....
....
....

4. When did you allow yourself to be vulnerable/to
   open up to others?

....

....

....

....

....

....

....

....

....

....

5. What are some of your happiest memories?

....

....

....

....

....

....

....

....

....

....

....

....

6. What is currently in your life that you are grateful to yourself for making happen?

....
....
....
....
....
....
....
....
....
....

SELF-CELEBRATION

Self-celebration means taking time to celebrate and reward yourself for your wins and achievements. It encourages us to pay attention to our efforts and to the ways in we which we show up for ourselves each day. It helps to boost self-esteem, cultivate self-love, and encourages us to direct our gratitude inward.

We live in a goal-oriented culture in which celebration tends to focus on only a select number of achievements: an engagement, buying a new home, a promotion, a new job, an award. We then get conditioned into thinking that everything else is not as worthy of recognition and acknowledgment. It can prevent us from seeing and appreciating all the incredible things we offer ourselves, and achieve, each and every day.

Get into the habit of celebrating not just milestones but progress, commitment, and effort. Congratulate yourself on the things you do, no matter how big or small: cooking a new recipe, completing a workout for the first time, honoring a boundary that you set, stepping out of your comfort zone, and reaching out to a potential client or putting yourself forward in a team meeting. **Get into the habit of paying attention to the small wins.**

How can we self-celebrate?

1. USE A MANTRA

When you have completed something you feel proud of, repeat a simple mantra to yourself such as "I am proud of my achievement," or "I am proud of the person I am today."

2. REWARD YOURSELF

Have you finally finished your assignment? Or spring-cleaned your house? Acknowledge it, sit with that feeling of accomplishment, and reward yourself in some way. That could mean carving out time for some self-care, booking a dinner at your favorite restaurant, or renting the latest blockbuster.

3. TELL SOMEONE

We often hold back from telling others when we feel proud of ourselves out of fear of sounding boastful. But self-celebration can be humble, inspiring, and uplifting: *I love hearing my friends share their high vibes with me!* I encourage you to start sharing your successes with the people in your life. Not only might it encourage them to do the same, but using self-affirming language out loud will help boost your self-esteem on a subconscious level too. *Win-win.*

4. JOURNAL

Every night before bed write down at least five things you did that day that you felt proud of, remembering that *no win is too small.*

GRATITUDE CHALLENGE

Every day this week send a message of gratitude to someone you are thankful for. It can be someone you know or it could be someone that has inspired you on social media. Let's spread the high vibes!

Write down the name of each person you will send a message to and tick it off as complete when you've sent the message.

Monday	☐
Tuesday	☐
Wednesday	☐
Thursday	☐
Friday	☐
Saturday	☐
Sunday	☐

STOP MOANING

So if gratitude is the feeling of appreciation, what is the antithesis? For me, it's *moaning*. I will be the first to admit that moaning was my second language. I would moan about everything; *I was what some people refer to as a Negative Nancy*. I would moan that the traffic was stressful, that the weather was awful, that the streets were too busy, the work was too hard, so-and-so was rude to me, I slept badly, and so on. The glass was always half empty, and I let everyone around me know it. In fact, if someone tried to offer me a more positive perspective, I would feel genuinely frustrated with them.

As I went deeper into my own manifesting process this changed. Moaning was replaced by appreciation, and *I* became the person trying to offer others a more empowering perspective. Healing my wounds, removing fear and doubt, becoming conscious of my language, and committing to my positivity journal (*see MANIFEST*) had rewired my pattern of thinking and I *naturally* began to see the glass as half full, and finding the silver lining in any challenging situation became my default. But, and this is important to say, **not always**. *I am not always feeling positive 100 percent of the time, and that is OK.* I lived for twenty-eight years behaving and thinking a certain way, and so it's not surprising that I occasionally slip into old patterns. This usually happens when I'm particularly stressed or when I'm just really exhausted. At such times my old friend Negative Nancy comes to join the party. I adopt a bit of a "poor me" attitude, and I know it. As soon as I recognize it, I make a conscious effort to change the tune because *it doesn't serve me*, it doesn't help me feel better, and it takes me away from the high-vibrational gratitude that I have retrained my mind to adopt.

I'm not saying that a little moan here and there is going to ruin your whole manifesting process. I mean, who doesn't feel better after calling their best friend to vent about their day at work? But *the habit* of moaning *is* an issue. For most of us, especially in Britain, moaning is a means of conversation and connection. Look at the conversations you have or overhear over the next few days and pay attention to how often people casually moan and use joint dissatisfaction to connect. *Why does it matter?* **The things we voice** out loud influence how we feel, what we believe, and therefore what we attract. Remember our subconscious, the place we manifest from, is always listening *and believing* whatever you say and consciously think. The more we say negative things (*i.e. moan*), the more we feel it, the lower we vibrate, and the less powerfully we attract abundance into our lives. For example, if you keep saying over and over again, "I am exhausted, I've had the worst day, I hate my boss, I can't stand the rain, I'm sick of the traffic, I have the worst luck," then because our subconscious cannot differentiate a truth from a lie, it will come to believe that life is really awful, and then we will keep attracting things into our life that support that narrative.

Every thought we have and every word we utter has an energetic effect that influences what we manifest into our lives.

When I was around fifteen, my older sister Noona came home from her NLP (neurolinguistic programming) course and told us that she had been learning about the influence that the language we use has on our mindset and well-being. She said that as part of her homework she was going to ban herself from complaining for five days. At the time I remember rolling my eyes, thinking, *Please, as if you're going to stick to that.* I can't remember what the result of that experiment was in the end, but the concept has always stayed with me.

When I notice myself falling back into the habit of moaning, I think about my sister's experiment and place myself under the same ban. It's remarkably simple: when I think about something I want to moan about, *I just don't*. I don't give the moaning a voice; instead I either say nothing at all or I think of a more uplifting perspective and more high-vibrational comment to say instead. For example, if I want to moan about how long a line is, I don't. When I want to moan about how rude somebody was to me, instead I say something like, "She must have been having a really bad day. I hope she feels better in herself later." When I stop voicing the negative, everything feels better. *Within a day* I feel more content and I can feel my vibe change with it. I break the cycle and bring myself back to a healthier mindset that helps to support my manifesting journey.

Try the moaning ban for yourself; set yourself a five-day target. See for yourself how much better you feel by the end and how quickly your mindset shifted. Then share the results on the Facebook group MANIFEST WITH ROXIE!

APPRECIATE THE ORDINARY

I've recently been reading *Regrets of the Dying* by Georgina Scull. In it the author interviews people who are either aged over eighty or have a terminal illness about regrets they have about their life. One story particularly moved me, a young girl named Tessa, who was just twenty-four when she was diagnosed with breast cancer which devastatingly became terminal. In the interview she said, *"When I die, I will miss taking deep breaths of fresh air, watching the sunset, and feeling the wind on my cheeks. I'll miss cuddles with my cat and the company of my partner. I will miss a cancer-free life. A chance to live the way I wanted. I will miss being alive."* I cried reading this.

Tessa's story and interview made me reflect on how much of the mundane we take for granted. When people are struck with grief, tragedy, or illness, it is so often the ordinary things they miss the most. The things we tend to take for granted and the moments we deem so insignificant. Since reading Georgina Scull's book, I have made an effort to pause and appreciate the ordinary, the mundane. When I cuddle Wolfe, I take mental snapshots, and when I am walking I pause for a few seconds to feel the breeze on my face and the sun kiss my skin and I whisper to myself, "I am grateful for all that I have." In *MANIFEST* I spoke of the importance of shifting your language from "I have to do it" to "*I get to do it*," and this feels even more relevant now. We get to be here, we get to experience life, we get to age, to make memories, and to live. **So let's make the most of this precious life that we have, this one shot we get at it. Don't waste it.**

➡ EXERCISE

I want you to keep a little diary for the next week. Fold
down the corner or leave a bookmark here so that each
day you can come back to this page. I want you to choose
three gloriously ordinary and mundane things that you are
deeply thankful for. When you are experiencing them, I
want you to focus on being mindful in those moments, by
taking a mental photograph, paying real attention to them,
and feeling your vibration change.

Day 1

1. . . . .

2. . . . .

3. . . . .

Day 2

1. . . . .

2. . . . .

3. . . . .

Day 3

1. . . . .

2. . . . .

3. . . . .

Day 4

1. . . . .
2. . . . .
3. . . . .

Day 5

1. . . . .
2. . . . .
3. . . . .

Day 6

1. . . . .
2. . . . .
3. . . . .

Day 7

1. . . . .
2. . . . .
3. . . . .

Manifesting is not just about attracting things into our lives, it is about making the best of the life we already have.

RAISE YOUR VIBRATION IN TWO MINUTES

Repeat these mantras out loud or inside your head five times.

I am worthy of receiving all the
abundance the universe has to offer.

I am ready to step into my light and
unlock my limitless potential.

I am excited for all the opportunities
that each new day brings.

I am grateful for all that I already have.

STEP 6
TURN ENVY INTO
INSPIRATION

"Comparison is the thief of joy."

THEODORE ROOSEVELT

OVERVIEW OF STEP 6

○ Envy is a low-vibrational emotion that stems from a scarcity mindset.
○ Inspiration is a high-vibrational emotion that stems from an abundance mindset.
○ We often try to deny and bury our envy rather than validating it.
○ The antithesis of envy is inspiration.
○ To let go of envy we must become aware of it, remove self-judgment around it, learn from it, and then turn it into inspiration.

I find envy to be such a fascinating emotion. When you feel it, it hits you hard. It brings with it a whole array of other emotions: sadness, fear, anger, bitterness, shame, guilt. It's unsurprising then that so many of us try to push it away, deny, or struggle to process it. But *we need to process it*. We need to learn to validate it and process it so that it does not lower our vibration and negatively impact our manifesting process.

Very simply, the first step to doing this is to become aware of envy and then to take ownership of it. When you feel it, I want you to admit it to yourself *without judgment*. For example, if you feel envious of your co-worker who got a promotion, or your friend who seems blissfully happy in her new relationship, or the person on your Instagram feed on holiday, pause and *say to yourself*, "I feel envious of this" or "Seeing/hearing this has made me feel envious." In stating how we feel we validate ourselves. When we validate ourselves, we offer ourselves the opportunity to understand, accept, process, and ultimately let go of the emotion.

Remember that at the heart of envy is fear. In Step 2: Remove Fear and Doubt I spoke about the importance of healing the wound and not the symptom, and this is applicable to this step too. **Envy is the symptom; fear is the wound.** Fear is born from our insecurity, low self-worth, and doubt. It is a fear that says someone else has something that I don't believe I am worthy or capable of having myself. This is what makes envy one of the most significant indicators of what within us still needs healing. It is what also makes *awareness around our envy* so integral to our ability to manifest what we want into our lives; only if we accept and validate our envy can we identify where our blocks (i.e. our fear and doubt) are.

As I said in *MANIFEST*, one of the most problematic things about denying envy is that we instead pass it on as judgment. Think about times you have judged or criticized somebody else. Do you think that you would feel compelled to do so if there wasn't a personal fear or feeling of lack that was driving it? For example, if you were to criticize somebody on social media for the way they express themselves, is a part of that driven by your own fear around expressing yourself authentically online?

Think about this: when a confident man or woman walks into a room, how often do people say, "Urgh, she's so arrogant," or "He's so cocky"? It's almost a knee-jerk reaction, but where does it come from? It's not coming from any factual evidence, because *confidence does not automatically equate to arrogance.* No, it comes from somewhere unhealed within that person, which triggers envy, envy of the confidence that they would like to possess more of. Consider for a moment *what someone who was truly confident within themselves would do when they watched someone else confidently walk into the room? They would feel totally unthreatened by it; they would celebrate it, respect it, be inspired by it.*

Passing judgment and criticizing others is so low-vibe. We must all, collectively, begin to practice non-judgment and **take ownership and responsibility for our perceptions of others.** If we don't get along with someone, or don't agree with them, we can simply be indifferent to them. That's OK, but being rude/critical/judgmental serves only to give our fears and doubts a voice that holds us back from abundance.

So when we accept and recognize that we are envious, what can we do to heal the wound it has come from? First we can offer ourselves compassion and a safe space for emotional expression. Second we can find a practical way to offer ourselves what we feel we are lacking. For example, let's say you are jealous or critical of people who dress in an expressive way. You might use that to help you recognize that you would like to have the confidence to express yourself more authentically. One practical way you could begin to bring that confidence to life might be to buy a small accessory that feels like a true expression of yourself. Or let's imagine you were secretly judging your friend who was always going on dates, and you recognized that it was a reflection of your own limiting belief that you were not worthy of attention or respect. You might decide to commit to a daily self-love ritual that allows you to show and build that love for yourself.

Rather than judging ourselves for feeling envious, or denying that we are experiencing it at all, we must use envy to help us on our manifesting journeys. Envy can show us parts of ourselves that need bringing to light so that we can clear our path to abundance.

⇛ EXERCISE

The prompts here are designed to help you explore your envy, heal it, and let it go. This work requires you to be vulnerable, open, and honest with yourself. *Watch out for the ego here; it will try to interfere and stop you from admitting your deepest fears and insecurities. Do not let it. We must bring them to light and expose them.* Do not judge yourself for what you are feeling or experiencing.

1. What or who do you feel envious of?

....
....

2. When have you disguised your envy as judgment or criticism of someone else?

....
....

3. What other emotions accompany the envy?

....
....

4. What wound is the envy guiding you to?

....
....

5. What is it revealing to you about yourself?

....
....

6. What would be a compassionate response to the wound that you could offer yourself now?

. . . .

. . . .

7. What practical steps can you take to heal the envy?

. . . .

. . . .

Envy is low-vibe and it is the antithesis of high-vibe inspiration. While envy reflects a scarcity mindset, inspiration reflects an abundant one. When we turn envy into inspiration, we turn that *low-vibe* response into a *high-vibe* one, enabling us to attract more abundance into our lives by the law of attraction. As with many other practices in this book, it is something we can train our brains to do. To do this we must first make a conscious effort to become aware of it and then actively replace an envious thought with an inspired one. For example, instead of saying, "I can't believe she got promoted; she didn't even deserve it," say to yourself, "I am happy for her success; I am so excited for how it will feel when I get promoted too."

Practice making this switch every time you feel envious and see how much better you feel instantly. Remember:

your subconscious will believe whatever you tell it. So say the inspired thought to yourself even if you don't quite believe it yet.

➡ EXERCISE

To really harness that feeling of inspiration (the antithesis of envy) and be able to use it on your manifesting journey, think about the people who you admire and then identify the qualities they possess that you would like to cultivate in yourself. Choose five people now and write down their names and inspiring qualities below:

1. ....
2. ....
3. ....
4. ....
5. ....

CELEBRATING OTHERS

Celebrating others is a demonstration of that high-vibrational supportive and abundant mindset. As you celebrate other people, you show the universe that you are not threatened by another person's success because you trust that there is enough love, happiness, and success for everyone. *If you believe in the abundance of the universe, you will receive abundance.*

I want to share a personal story with you that I think is a perfect demonstration of this. I was going through my archived Instagram stories from November 2019 to find some stories from my first-ever workshop, which was on the theme of self-love. I came across a story I had posted three days afterward. It was posted to celebrate my friend Tori, who had started a crystal bracelet brand over the lockdown, called TBalance. The supermodel Bella Hadid was pictured wearing it and Tori had shared it on her social media. I absolutely love Bella Hadid and have for *years*. Not only is she breathtakingly beautiful, but I also think she is an incredible mental health advocate, and her authentic passion to fight for and support what she believes in is admirable. I remember feeling so excited for Tori when I saw her share the picture. I reposted the picture on my own Instagram and I wrote, *So incredibly proud of my incredible soulful @tbalance_crystals whose amazing bracelet that I wear every day is being worn by my fashion idol @bellahadid. They're such beautiful pieces. Check out her website!* I was not threatened by my friend's success; I was inspired by it and I celebrated it. Then, two years later, supermodel Bella Hadid stepped out of her New York apartment proudly holding my orange book, *MANIFEST: 7 Steps to Living Your Best Life*, under her arm for the world to see. I mean, seriously, *what are the chances?* I felt like this was such a gift from the universe, a reward for that high-vibrational support and celebration of another woman.

I want to challenge you to actively celebrate others' success. That might be by shouting about it on your social media, sending them a text to say how proud you are of them, emailing someone to let them know how much they inspired you, or just by leaving a comment under their post the next time they share something they are proud of. **Let's get into the habit of lifting each other up and raising our collective vibration.**

DEALING WITH COMPARISON

We live in a **culture of comparison**. Social media platforms and dating apps have become a huge part of our lives and the impact they have on our self-worth must not be underestimated. They provide us with a constant source of comparison, allowing our limiting beliefs and insecurities to be constantly fed and fueled. We compare our wardrobes, our jobs, our friendships, our looks, our relationships, and our financial status to the perfectly curated profiles that pop up on our feeds, and then we wonder why we find it so hard to appreciate all that we already have. We seem to have this strange bias: even though we have so much of our own lives and stories that we don't share, we assume that someone else's life is exactly how they represent it on social media. We forget that behind every picture is another story of struggle, hard work, or sacrifice. It's as though we see somebody's Instagram profile, seeing just the parts of themselves they want us to see, and then our minds fill in the gaps and create an idealized image of who that person is and how they live day-to-day. And then we compare that image, that imagined reality, to our own lives.

It's not just on social media that we compare ourselves, though, of course. We compare ourselves to our friends, our siblings, our peers. We even compare ourselves to celebrities. I remember being twenty-five and feeling like I had absolutely nothing to show for myself, and watching Taylor Swift on stage at Hyde Park, absolutely mesmerized by her performance and her success, thinking, *I can't believe she is the same age as me.*

Comparison harbors envy and holds you back from your manifestations. It triggers limiting beliefs, low self-worth, and the insecurity that lives unhealed within us. **Comparing yourself to others does nothing but distract you from where you are heading and drain your precious time and energy.**

If you want to be the best version of yourself and if you want to manifest your very best life, then do this: *stay in your own lane and keep laser-sharp focus on your own journey.* Think about it like this: imagine you were racing the four-hundred-meter sprint. If you kept looking over at the person running next to you, no doubt you would stumble, fall back, and lose time. So to run the sprint in your best-possible time you have to keep your eyes on the finish line and not, even for a second, look over at anyone else.

In one of my workshops I had a question from a lady in the audience who wanted to start her own bedding company. She was apprehensive because she felt that the market was saturated and that made her feel afraid that she wouldn't be able to succeed, because what if she couldn't compare to the other brands in the same field? I said this, "The fact that the market is saturated means that there is a demand for it. See that as a good sign. Then focus not on trying to compare yourself to any other brand, but on finding what makes your brand so authentic that it offers something totally different and unique."

I experienced my own version of this recently. I was looking at the social media accounts of renowned coaches and speakers, ones that I personally admire, and I began to notice that the vast majority of their content was focused on their message. There was little on their pages about their personal lives, or lifestyles, but instead they offered a constant resource of inspiring content, with self-development tips and speeches and videos. I started to compare my own page to theirs. I thought, *Oh no, mine is so personal. I share so much lifestyle, fashion, skincare. Does that make me less credible? Will people take me less seriously as a manifesting expert or self-development coach? Should I change what I share?* I had to remind myself that I'm not here to be like anyone else;

I'm just here to be me and trust that *that is enough*. And for me, I love sharing my life—I wouldn't *want* to give that up—and I hope that in doing so I can show that self-development and fashion, wellness, popular culture, travel, and skincare can all go hand in hand. We all allow comparison to trigger self-doubt, but you can choose whether you allow that to fuel envy or a more empowering perspective.

We are so quick to compare ourselves to others, yet when do we ever compare the other people in our lives against each other? Just think about the people closest to you, or the people you identified above that you are inspired by. Have you ever thought to yourself, *I love my best friend, but she's not as outgoing as my other friend, so maybe I should respect or love her a little less?* No, of course you haven't; that would be absurd. You love this friend for all her wonderful uniqueness, for her nuances, for who she is on her best days and her worst. That's how you should be thinking about yourself.

The truth is this: whatever anyone else is doing is none of your concern. The only comparison you should be making is who you are today with who you were yesterday and who you want to be tomorrow. Your job is not to be more like someone else but to be the best of you. That is how you harness magnetic authenticity and attract the people and things in your life that are truly aligned with *who you really are.*

STEP 7

TRUST IN THE UNIVERSE

"I don't chase, I attract."

UNKNOWN

OVERVIEW OF STEP 7

○ Trusting the universe means knowing what you
want and then having unwavering faith that it *will*
manifest itself into your life.

○ This trust is a "knowing feeling." You don't know
how; you just know that it will.

○ Unwavering confidence is magnetic.

○ Manifesting is not about control; it's about
surrender.

○ You have to let go of waiting and not let impatience
interfere with divine timing.

○ Trust is the glue that holds all the steps of
manifesting together.

To ultimately call what we want to manifest into our
lives we must leave no room for doubt or uncertainty to
exist. We must harness full faith and trust in the universe
and allow that magnetic confidence to fuel our manifesting power.

One way that we can begin to build that trust, from this
moment, is to acknowledge and recognize that we have all
already been manifesting in some way or another for our

whole lives. The way we have been thinking, acting, and behaving has been influencing our experiences; there will have been times in your life when you were unintentionally practicing the seven steps and attracting abundance into your life, and there will have been times in your life when you woke up in a terrible mood and spilled coffee all over yourself.

✏️ EXERCISE

I want you to reflect on the times in your life when you can recognize, in hindsight, that you were unknowingly manifesting. It might have been a time when you just absolutely knew, without doubt, that you were going to get that job. Or it might have been a time when you were thinking about an old friend and then you bumped into them the very next day. Perhaps it's a time when you said, "I can't believe what a coincidence this is," only now you see that it wasn't a coincidence at all but the universe responding to you—*manifesting in disguise*. Try to think of as many examples as you can.

Times in my life I have unknowingly manifested . . .

....

....

....

....

....

....

....

....

....

....

....

....

....

....

....

....

....

....

....

....

....

....

....

....

As you look over what you have written, allow that feeling of faith and trust in the universe to strengthen. You can see now, from your own experiences, that it is always listening, watching, and responding to what you do.

SURRENDER

Surrender is such an important part of this step, and of the entire manifesting process. To surrender is to let go of control, to have acceptance, and to allow things to unfold as they are supposed to. It is the opposite of trying to force something or to will it desperately into existence. To me *surrender is high-vibrational, while control is low-vibrational.* I always think of it like this: have you ever got into the car, perhaps a bit frustrated, and tried to pull down on your seat belt to fasten it, but when you pull it you try a little too hard—you're too forceful and the seat belt just locks shut; it doesn't move. You have to ease off; you have to gently pull it down, slowly, without force, and only then will it work for you so that you can fit it into place. That's like manifesting. The more we try to force things into place, the more we disrupt the energetic flow. We interrupt divine timing and we take away from that high-vibrational trust and faith that will ultimately lead us to where we want to go.

How do we learn to surrender? We practice it every day. I speak to Wade all the time about the concept of surrender as it is at the center of his own self-development journey. He told me that learning to surrender was one of the most profound and transformative experiences of his life. I said to him, "But what are you surrendering to?" He said, "*I surrender to what is.*"

I asked Wade to expand on this and this is what he expressed to me: "The more deeply I surrender to what is actually happening in any given moment, the more at peace I feel. I often consider one of Buddha's four noble truths when I'm working with surrender—that the cause of suffering is desire. I interpret this for myself as meaning that any time I have an expectation or preference as to how things should be, I set myself up for disappointment. Because, of course, life isn't going to unfold exactly the way I expect it to. I heard a great quote from Russell Brand where he said that 'expectation is just another word for fantasy.' So I now try to catch myself every time I'm constructing a fantasy about how I need things to be, and instead I try to relax into how things really are. I focus my energy on being completely present with what *is*. I find that the more I practice this, the more comfortable I have become with trusting the universe. I keep letting go of life needing to unfold in any specific way at all, and I just try to accept and embrace what it is. This doesn't take me further away from what I want—it brings me closer. And it means that my journey in getting there is one that is filled with a much deeper sense of joy. It means

I gain access to feeling at peace no matter what happens, because I have truly let go of my expectations as to how my life should be. Life is like a river; rather than having to control every twist and turn, instead embrace the flowing journey that you are on and give thanks that the universe is guiding the way."

Begin to practice surrender each and every day and demonstrate your unwavering faith in the universe by relaxing into and accepting what is. Start by becoming acutely aware of your expectations. Next time you catch yourself coming up with a story about how things should be, pause, take a deep breath, and let it go. Similarly, if you find yourself disappointed or upset that something has happened in a way you didn't expect, take a second to pause, accept, breathe, and surrender to the experience. The beautiful by-product of practicing surrender in this way is that you also cultivate that high-vibrational attitude of gratitude, because your focus shifts to what you have (*what is*) and not what you lack (*what isn't*).

> THERE IS A MANTRA THAT I LOVE TO RE-PEAT AT TIMES WHEN I NEED HELP TO SUR-RENDER. IT GOES, "I ALLOW THINGS TO UNFOLD AS THEY ARE SUPPOSED TO WITH-OUT EXPECTATION."

Whether we are conscious of it or not, we all have a set of personal preferences and expectations that dictate the way we want our lives to be. We have already decided, in our minds, how we would like our partners and friends to behave, how we want our careers to progress, and how we want to be perceived by others. Think about it like this: have you ever gone to have a "serious talk" with a partner or colleague? Before meeting them how many times did you play out an imagined conversation of what you would say, how they would respond, and so on? Now consider how often those conversations *actually* go as you had envisaged them.

We do this when we embark on a manifesting journey too; for example, let's say you want to manifest your dream job. You have clarity on the exact job you want, you believe you are worthy of it, and you feel as though you have worked through the rest of the steps. But deep down you have also decided *exactly how* you want things to happen: on the path to your dream job you don't want to have to deal with too many job interviews, any rejection; you don't want to have to sacrifice your party lifestyle and you certainly don't want to have to wait for too long before that job offer comes through. *All these preferences and expectations only serve to show the universe that you aren't willing to relinquish control at all.* When the path to your manifestation doesn't go as you expected, you lose faith and are much more likely to give up on your goals altogether.

When you aren't truly ready to surrender you send a message to the universe that says you are still being restricted by your fear and doubt.

The constant expectation of how we want the future to play out stops us from accepting what is. We miss out on so many beautiful experiences, because we get so caught up in the disappointment of our expectations not having been met. For example, imagine it rains on our holiday when we had expected sunshine every day. When that happens, we miss out on the joy of simply being somewhere new without the stresses of work. We need to accept what is so that we can embrace life, be present in our experiences, and ride the waves of life with greater ease.

To truly trust in the universe we need to be able to let go of all the ways in which we would like things to happen and all the expectations we have about how life should unfold. We need to have unwavering faith that what we want to manifest will come to us, while surrendering to the journey that will lead us there.

For some of us the idea of surrender can still feel counter-intuitive to the proactive nature of manifestation. To clarify, **manifesting is about knowing what you want and then letting that go.** You aren't required to focus day in and day out on your goals, and you don't need to either, because after creating your vision board and regularly practicing visualization meditations, your subconscious will get to work on getting you there. **What you do need to do, day-to-day, is:** align your behavior with your future, and work on inner healing, cultivating self-love, immersing yourself in gratitude, and becoming the best version of yourself that exists. Focus your attention on *that* and not on *how* it's going to happen.

Surrender can support almost every step of the manifesting journey. In Step 1: Be Clear in Your Vision we must surrender to infinite possibilities when identifying how we want our lives to feel and look. We cannot get in our heads thinking, *But how will it happen? How realistic is that?* No, **we must surrender all disbelief and dare to dream.** In Step 2: Remove Fear and Doubt we must surrender ourselves to our healing journeys. We must trust that if we allow ourselves the space and time to process our past traumas, and if we come to it with vulnerability and openness, we will remove blocks that will help us to unlock the abundance of the universe. In Step 3: Align Your Behavior we must surrender ourselves as we step outside our comfort zones, throwing caution to the wind as we take the risks required to reach the next level. In Step 4: Overcome Tests from the Universe we must surrender completely to accept that the things that did not work out were not meant for us. We must trust that when things fall apart they are really falling together. We must surrender too as we let go of all that no longer serves us. In Step 5:

Embrace Gratitude (Without Caveats) we must surrender ourselves to the present so that we can appreciate all that we already have and sink into that high-vibrational feeling of appreciation. In Step 6: Turn Envy into Inspiration we must surrender our tendency for comparison and trust that sticking in our own lane will lead us to where we want to go. And here, in Step 7: Trust in the Universe, we must surrender to the unfolding of our life.

EPILOGUE

TO MANIFEST:
To make something happen

Whenever I get asked, "What exactly is manifesting?" I say this: "**Manifesting is the ability to use the power of your mind to change and create the reality you experience. It is a self-development practice to live by.**" To me manifesting is the umbrella of self-development, and all self-help and inner healing falls beneath it. It is why I believe it can help to empower and transform the lives of each and every person that practices it.

Manifesting is not this mystical fluffy practice that some people think it is. It's not just about positive thinking or visualizing what you want. It's not about a constant pursuit of more, more, more. It's not a ritual that you do for twenty minutes a day. **Manifesting is a way of living. It is about unlocking the most powerful, magnetic, and confident version of yourself that exists so that *you can make things happen*.** It's about making the life you have feel the best that it can be. It isn't magic at all, but the results of it *feel* magical.

215

Remember: these steps aren't done one after the other but simultaneously. Each step feeds and supports the others. Allow them to become a guide to support how you govern yourself and your life.

MAKE LIVING YOUR BEST LIFE A NON-NEGOTIABLE

When you are crystal clear on the person you want to be and you are proactive in making your dreams a reality by taking risks, stepping outside your comfort zone, committing to your healing journey, and cultivating self-love in everything that you do, manifesting your best life should be non-negotiable. When you talk about your future, do not leave room for doubt. *There are no "ifs," there is only "when."* Do not stop until you get there. If one door shuts, open another. Someone very dear to me used to always tell me, "There are a million ways to get to the same point," which means if it doesn't work out the first time you try or the route you take doesn't lead you there, find another route, try another way. Never settle for a life that is less than what you truly desire and deserve.

I live and breathe these seven steps; they feed into absolutely everything that I do, and they empower me to live a life of contentment, fulfillment, joy, and abundance. I hope that after reading my MANIFEST books, you can understand how limitless you really are, and how much power you hold within you. I hope you have started to uncover your most authentic self and begun to heal all the wounds that life has left you with. I hope that you start to really *believe* the truth: **that you are enough, that you have always been enough, and that you deserve to live a life that makes you feel excited to get out of bed each day.** You are worthy of all the happiness, love, success, and abundance that the universe has to offer. I really wish I could have told my younger self what I want to tell you now:

LIFE IS WONDERFUL AND YOU HAVE THE POWER TO MAKE IT SO.

ACKNOWLEDGMENTS

To Wolfe

Thank you for bringing endless joy and love into my life. Being your mum is the greatest honor of my life.

To Paula

Thank you being there for me in my darkest times and celebrating with me in the best times, too. Delo face forever.

To Simon & Andrew

Thank you for being in the rocket ship with me and for your endless love and support.

To all of you

Thank you, from the bottom of my heart, for letting me into your journeys, for trusting in my seven steps, and for sharing the power of manifestation with those around you. I am so proud and grateful for this incredible community. Together we are making a real difference in this world. I love you all!

SOURCES

p. 39. Brené Brown, "Striving versus Self-Acceptance, Saving Marriages, and More (#409)," *The Tim Ferris Show*, podcast, February 6, 2020

p. 60. Rebecca Solnit, *Men Explain Things to Me*, Granta, 2014

p. 86. Anaïs Nin, *Seduction of the Minotaur*, Swallow Press, 1961

p. 104. Steve Maraboli, *Life, the Truth, and Being Free*, Better Today Publishing, 2010

INDEX

Hadid, Bella 198–9
happiness 12–15, 115, 170,
  172–4
heartbreak 152–3
high-vibe/high-vibrational
  frequency 5, 26, 58,
  161, 170, 188,
  196, 208
hobbies 21, 92
home 9–10, 17
honesty 23–4

I
imposter syndrome
  1, 78–9
inner critic 64, 87, 97
inner-child meditation
  46–52
insecurity 150
inspiration 139, 148, 191,
  196–9, 214
Islam 169

J
Jeffers, Susan 115
journaling 29, 50–1,
  139, 180
  for healing 43–6
joy 172
judgment
  fear of 84–5
  and the need to be
    liked 91–3

L
lateness 113–14
laziness 115, 131
leisure 17, 21, 110
letting go 72, 152–5, 165
  of envy 191–7
limiting 156
love 17, 21, 48
  conditional 85
  of self see self-love
low-vibe/low-vibrational
  frequency 5, 23, 43, 53,
  196
  and energy protection
    161–4
luck 156, 183

M
MANIFEST: 7 Steps to
  Living Your Best Life 1–2,
  78–9, 94, 105, 120, 198
manifesting
  and being proactive
    105
  blocks to 59
  definition 215
  supporting your
    journey 139–40
  tests to overcome
    143–4, 148–9
  understanding what
    you want 11–14
  unknowingly 206

225

NOTES

....
....
....
....
....
....
....
....
....
....
....
....
....
....
....
....
....
....
....
....
....
....
....

NOTES

NOTES